SECRET WAR

BLITZ EDITIONS

Published by Blitz Editions
an imprint of Bookmart Ltd
Registered Number 2372865
Trading as Bookmart Ltd
Desford Road
Enderby
Leicester LE9 5AD

ISBN 1 85605 266 4

PICTURE CREDITS

The publisher would like to thank the following organisations for supplying photographs for use in this book.
Every effort has been made to contact the copyright holders for the pictures. In some cases they have been untraceable, for which we offer our apologies.

Hulton Deutsch; Imperial War Museum; US National Archives; Robert Hunt Library; Norsk Hydro; The Public Archives of Canada; Associated Press; State of Israel Government Press Office; Embassy of The Federal Republic of Germany; Nato Photo; UN Photo; EEC London; US Library of Congress; J Baker Collection; Bundesarchiv; BFI; National Film Archive; Truman Library; Tanjug.

THE AUTHOR

Karen Farrington is a writer and former Fleet Street journalist who has specialised in the study of conflict throughout the 20th Century. In compiling Witness to World War II she has personally interviewed scores of veterans from around the world, obtaining a unique insight into the war through the eyes of the men on the front line. Among her previous books is 'Fated Destiny', an historical pot pourri of the curious, shocking and mysterious which includes accounts of some of the greatest military blunders in recent history. Karen Farrington is married with three children and lives in Exmoor, Devon.

This book was produced by Amazon Publishing Limited
Designed by Wilson Design Associates

Printed in the Czech Republic
51761

Secret War

SPY ACTIVITY

The risky business of spying has excited and intrigued people for generations. It has been the source of novels, films and gossip for years. Those armchair experts who rely on Ian Fleming and Graham Greene – themselves ex-intelligence men – for their information drink in every detail of espionage and how it works. Those in the know generally keep quiet.

During World War II, spying was more thrilling than any book and more daring than any movie. Spies were motivated by nationalism, ideology, a fierce sense of right and wrong, love, lust or simply cash. Those who were caught in action paid with their lives – or abruptly switched loyalties. Luckier spies who survived rarely saw their names in lights.

The groundwork carried out by agents during the war was of almost inestimable value to the governments for which they worked.

In Britain, spies were controlled by the Special Operations Executive. In America, the Office of Strategic Services was set up in June 1942.

Yet not all the authorities were quick to realise the value of what was being presented to them.

CICERO

The information passed on by Cicero, the spy they didn't believe, is a classic case of a missed opportunity by the Germans.

Cicero was in fact an Albanian by the name of Elyesa Bazna. He worked at the British embassy in Ankara, Turkey first as a servant then as a valet. It seems that the ambassador, Sir Hughe Knatchbull-Hugessen, was very lackadaisical in matters of security.

Even the untrained eye of the valet appreciated that the chances to rifle through top secret papers were too frequent to miss. Bazna decided to make some extra cash by selling the secrets that he found lying around his master's bedroom to the Germans.

Bazna set about his task of photographing papers during evenings when Knatchbull-Hugessen was elsewhere. His booty included a list of Allied agents working in Turkey, confidential minutes of many top level conferences, details of diplomatic code and even the plans for the forthcoming invasion of Europe, codenamed 'Operation Overlord'.

To the delight of the German spymasters in the region who named him 'Cicero', the information just kept coming. So valuable was the link that documents from the ambassador's boudoir were sent straight to Joachim von Ribbentrop in Berlin for assessment at the highest level.

Strangely enough, von Ribbentrop dismissed 'Cicero' out of hand as a hoaxer. He could not believe that a mere servant would have access to such highly classified information.

Moreover, he decided Cicero's claims to be anti-British after his father had been shot by an Englishman were dubious. For one thing, Bazna spoke excellent English; for another, he kept changing his story, and neither fact did much to enhance his credibility with the Germans. Von Ribbentrop suspected he had been planted by the British themselves. Franz von Papen, the German ambassador to Turkey, was instructed to disregard the information received through this channel.

Documents went straight to von Ribbentrop for assessment at the highest level

Little did Hitler's Foreign Minister realise the woeful lack of security at the British embassy.

Germany's spymasters were outraged at von Ribbentrop's attitude, and continued to find the cash to finance Cicero, despite opposition from Berlin. Cicero apparently operated between October 1943 and March 1944. Then, the British were tipped off about his covert activities and began their own investigations. It took them a long time to plug the leak because it came from the ambassador's residence, rather than from the embassy as had long been suspected.

Cicero was forewarned of the risk by Germany and fled with £300,000 in counterfeit British notes. The fake payment by the Germans resulted in Bazna languishing for some time in a Turkish prison after he had tried to use them. In 1962, now living in

Opposite: **Franz von Papen was Hitler's ambassador to Turkey when Cicero's secrets began to filter through.**
Below: **Radio transmitters like those carried by spies Joseph Waldberg and Karl Meier when they entered Britain posing as refugees: they were arrested.**

Above: **The original offices in central London which housed Special Operations Executive, the heartbeat of Britain's espionage activities.**

Germany and working as a night watchman, Bazna wrote a book called 'I was Cicero'.

There has been speculation since the war that von Ribbentrop was right to have his suspicions because 'Cicero' was in fact a successful double agent working for the British. Convenient as it might be for the British to appear on top of the matter, it seems the conspiracy theory is probably only bunkum. Almost certainly, there was a criminal lack of security at the British embassy that endangered Allied activities throughout Europe. Sir Hughe was quietly moved to another diplomatic posting without appearing to suffer so much as a reprimand.

One of the greatest of the German security scoops during World War II came when they asserted full control over intelligence operations out of Holland. Their canny grasp of the system cost the lives of hundreds of Dutch and British agents.

They stole a march on Holland early in the war. Two accomplished Nazi agents posed as plotters against Hitler and made secret contact with Britain.

Two Britons, Major Richard Stevens and Captain Zigismund Payne Best, met the men claiming to be Captain Schaemmel of the transport corps and Captain Hausmann, an army medic, first in Arnhem and then in Venlo, on the Dutch-German border.

One of the Germans was in fact Walter Schellenberg, a notorious spy now being used to discover if the British were party to any genuine anti-Nazi plots. His carefully laid subterfuge went awry when a bomb exploded in a Munich beer cellar, clearly aimed at Hitler who narrowly escaped with his life. Believing it to be a British plot, Hitler wanted revenge.

So when Stevens, Best and a Dutch agent arrived for a rendezvous at Venlo, three carloads of armed SS men were waiting for them. The Dutch agent was shot dead while the Britons were bundled into a car and taken to Berlin for interrogation.

Talks that had been taking place through the Vatican were now abandoned by the British who saw new security risks. And when the Germans marched into Holland and France in 1940, they seized details of the secret agent networks from the Allied embassies.

By the summer of 1940, the British secret service channels in Europe were in shreds

By summer 1940, the British secret service in Europe was in shreds. As one chief put it: 'We did not possess one single agent between the Balkans and the English Channel.'

Germany, meanwhile, was piling on the pressure. A team of agents was parachuted into Britain, but most of them were easily identified by their amateurish approach.

The Germans also used men like George Owens, a Welsh engineer, recruited as a subversive by the Abwehr to whip up domestic disharmony and promote the Nazi cause. When Owens was caught by the British, he switched allegiance and began sending fake messages to Berlin under the guidance of MI5. It was the first step on a long road for Britain in her attempt to win the secret war.

DOUBLE AGENT

Germany continued its attempts to undermine the British through the use of agents. One of their biggest coups was to recruit Christiaan Lindemans, thought to be a hero of the Dutch resistance but in fact a double agent in the pay of the Nazis.

Lindemans was arrested on 28 October 1944. Following an interrogation by MI5 in London he was returned to Dutch custody where he languished until July 1946 when he committed suicide.

Ex-wrestler Lindemans was a strapping man who went by the codename King Kong. He had offered his services to the British in 1944 to help Allied servicemen escape from the occupied territory.

He had no problem getting security clearance, and then he set about his task with enthusiasm.

D-Day was followed by the march through Europe and the battle for Antwerp. Britain's Field Marshal Bernard Montgomery hoped to break the battle deadlock with 'Operation Market Garden', in which parachute regiments were sent into Arnhem to capture key bridges from the Germans and assist the thrust forward. When the paras landed they found to their surprise and horror that the area was already held by crack German troops. One division was pinned down and suffered horrendous casualties.

It has been suggested that Lindemans was a double agent on the Allied side

There was speculation that the plan had been betrayed, and the prime suspect was later thought to be Lindemans. This suggestion has largely been rejected on the grounds that the Wehrmacht could judge for itself that a major airborne operation was imminent simply by the weight of radio traffic that September. Also, it is thought unlikely that Lindemans was privy to the necessary information.

In Lindemans' defence, it has been suggested that he was in fact a double agent whose loyalties remained true to the Allies even while he was briefing the Germans. He was then sacrificed to expediency.

Whatever the facts of the Lindemans affair, it was certainly true that while Britain triumphed in the spying game elsewhere, in Holland they came a poor second.

Germany had its fair share of agents at work in the heart of the Allied war effort. Among them were Nazi sympathisers at the American embassy in London who spent their time copying Churchill's secret telegrams to Roosevelt. Spycatcher Joan Miller helped to stem this gushing leak.

Yet internal rivalry between the Abwehr, the military intelligence branch which considered Nazis to be thuggish and undesirable, and the SD, Hitler's own security machine, would ultimately hamper the effectiveness of operations.

BARBAROSSA

Russia, meanwhile, had a thriving network of spies most of whom were inspired to pass on what secrets they could through their loyalty to the communist cause.

It was thanks to this somewhat blind devotion that Stalin was so well-informed about the Nazi

Below: **Sir Hughe Knatchbull-Hugessen with his wife and daughters. He was guilty of slack security when he was Britain's ambassador to Turkey.**

EYE WITNESS

Edward Howe was a former foreign correspondent who was recruited for the Special Operations Executive in 1943 to cultivate contacts with the resistance movements of Hungary and Yugoslavia.

'Someone told our august military hierarchy that I knew Hungary quite well. I was asked if I would help. Would I put myself in their hands? Somehow, they said, they would get me into Hungary so that I could report on conditions there.

This meant changing the War Correspondent tabs on my shoulder for three pips. The change caused me one embarrassment. I found it hard to salute smartly. Fortunately, I was not in Cairo – the only place it mattered – very long.

After two months training in the winter of 1943 I was considered ready to drop into Yugoslavia whence Partisans would pass me on towards Hungary. That was the plan. Things turned out differently.

Bad weather and German activity delayed my drop into Yugoslavia for two months. It took five flights and about 40 operational flying hours before I touched down in the Majevica hills bordering the River Sava.

It is a nerve-wracking business waiting in the fuselage of the aeroplane before being dropped by parachute. You do not know where you are or what is happening and it is extremely uncomfortable.

The crew are too busy with their own jobs to take much interest in you and it is impossible to keep up a conversation in a warplane.

So you sit quietly and anxiously in the darkness. Or rather you crouch, for your only seat is the bundles of supplies destined to follow you to the ground. On your back you wear your parachute fitted before you enter. It must not be taken off until the operation is declared unsuccessful and the plane has turned back.

With 28lb of costly silk on your back, a comfortable position is hard to find. But the physical discomfort is nothing compared to the mental anguish.

My feelings when the missions were abandoned were mixed, disappointment, a little relief. There is always some relief in the postponement of danger. But then there is the thought that I should have to go through all this again.'

Left: **Walter Schellenberg was probably Germany's most accomplished spy. His covert activities helped control the intelligence network in Holland.**

'Operation Barbarossa'. Nevertheless, he chose to ignore the warnings that a Nazi invasion of Russia was imminent.

The German Richard Sorge was one of the communist sympathisers who betrayed his country to Russia. A clerk at the German embassy in Tokyo, he regularly passed on classified information to Moscow. With Japan having now joined with Germany and Italy in the Tripartite Pact, top grade security information was being processed through the embassy. Sorge ensured that the best of it was passed to the Kremlin. This impeccable source was silenced when Sorge was caught spying and killed.

Also working for Moscow was the Lucy Ring in Switzerland. This was a cell made up of three committed communists who fed Stalin top-notch information from early 1942 until October 1943 when Swiss police, acting under pressure from Germany, broke up the network they knew as 'Rote Drei' (Red Three).

For nearly two years, the Lucy Ring in Switzerland fed about 140 messages a month to Russia

LUCY RING

The trio were Bavarian anti-Nazi Rudolf Roessler, Hungarian Sandor Rado and Englishman Alexander Foote. Foote was arrested as soon as he aroused suspicion. Roessler was taken into Swiss custody on 2 June 1944 and Rado went into hiding until the war ended.

It is still uncertain how and where this cell obtained its information.

At the height of its activity, the Lucy Ring was generating about 140 messages a month to Russia. So efficient was it that information was passed on sometimes within a matter of hours of crucial meetings held in Berlin. German Chief of General Staff Franz Halder later said: 'Almost every offensive operation of ours was betrayed to the enemy even before it appeared on my desk.'

The information passed to Russia during this period was so accurate

Above: **Mystery still surrounds the source of the information gathered by Rudolf Roessler and his associates in the so-called Lucy Ring.**

that even the Kremlin became suspicious about its provenance. Soviet spymasters continually pressed for the sources to be unmasked but they apparently were never divulged to the Kremlin. Time and time again, the codenames Werther, Teddy, Olga and Anna appeared as the informers.

Theories about their identities have been legion. One book claimed they were all friends made by Roessler in World War I in the army who had since achieved high rank in the Wehrmacht and were dismayed at the excesses of their Führer.

Another suggestion is that Swiss intelligence fed the Lucy Ring despite the country's fierce neutrality. There was fear that as Germany swept through Europe it would submerge little Switzerland, and it was in the interests of the independent Swiss state to ensure that Russia was given a fighting chance in the conflict so as to lessen the risk to its own security.

A third proposition is that the Lucy Ring was under the control of the British. Happily, Britain had virtually all the enemy's secrets thanks to the code-cracking Ultra system. Although Stalin was distrusted despite being one of the Allies, Churchill wanted to give the Red Army every advantage in its fight against Hitler, so it may be that information gleaned from Ultra was funnelled directly to the Russians through the Lucy Ring.

Two teleprinter operators in Germany who were deeply involved in an anti-Nazi conspiracy also came under the spotlight. Rado himself endorsed this theory.

CANARIS

Foote, who was an agent for Moscow until he defected back to Britain in 1947, died in 1956. Despite the services he rendered, Rado spent 10 years in a labour camp in Russia following the war. With both Rado and Roessler now long dead too, it seems unlikely the mystery of Lucy's impeccable sources will ever be revealed.

The Allies became well practised in the art of espionage and won some notable successes. Perhaps their greatest coup was to receive help from Admiral Wilhelm Canaris, one-time head of the German Abwehr.

Canaris was a patriotic German who, like many people, was filled with disgust for Hitler and his abuses of power. That he was a leading figure in the German resistance which hoped to overthrow Hitler has long been established. By 1951, the speculation about his role as an agent for Britain was rife.

Admiral Canaris was a patriotic German disgusted by Hitler's abuses of power

Yet it was not until 40 years after the end of the war that MI6 officer Andrew King confirmed to the Sunday Times that Canaris had passed on secrets to London through an emissary.

His link was Halina Szymanski, wife of a Polish Colonel who lived out the war in Switzerland. Canaris met a grisly end, being strangled with piano wire by the vengeful SS in reprisal for the July 1944 bomb plot against Hitler.

American-born Eric Erickson, a Swedish citizen and international oil dealer, was one of the free world's most successful spies. It was his information about oil installations around the Third Reich that provided valuable assistance to the bombers of both Britain and America. Their repeated

LONG KNIVES

When Hitler won power as Reich Chancellor in 1933, he set about eradicating opposition not only among those of different ideologies but those that shared the same callous creed as himself. His targets were the Brownshirts, internal paramilitaries who had played no small part in promoting the cause of Nazism through their bully-boy tactics on the streets of Germany.

At their head was Ernst Roehm, an ageing soldier who fashioned the Brownshirts – otherwise known as the Sturmabteilung or SA – after himself. They were brutal, ruthless, sadistic and many were openly homosexual.

Hitler had a long-standing friendship with Roehm which he was loath to betray. But, wary of the increasing power of the Brownshirts and the excesses in their behaviour, he felt he had no choice in the matter. On 30 June 1934 he sparked the beginning of the Night of the Long Knives. An estimated 200 died in 48 hours after henchmen worked their way through a list of Reich 'enemies'. Gregor Strasser, Hitler's one-time rival for the leadership of the Nazi party and Roehm himself, were among the victims.

Rudolf Hess alone among Hitler's inner circle was appalled at the bloodshed and argued long and hard for reprieves for names on the list. Others, including Himmler and Göring, appeared to relish the massacre, and were confident that it was consolidating their own grip on power.

attacks finally helped to throttle the Fatherland which was unable to maintain its war effort without fuel.

Erickson had frequently travelled to Germany before the outbreak of war, spoke the language fluently and was a noted anti-Nazi. When he was offered a chance to bring down Hitler by working undercover for Britain and, later, the Allies, he didn't hesitate.

It meant undergoing a public personality change. No longer did he attack Fascist policies at every opportunity. Now he trumpeted their cause and defended their actions.

ERIC ERICKSON

Although it cost him many of his friends, by September 1941 Erickson had won the permit he needed to enter Germany.

Once there, he had to undergo questioning from the Gestapo, a crucial test of his new pro-Nazi identity. Cool and collected, Erickson persuaded the grim-faced security men that his passion for Hitler was genuine. Soon he was being taken on a conducted tour of German oil fields because he had convinced the Nazis that he was there to buy some for his own country.

Only two people in Sweden knew about his mission. One was his new wife Ingrid. The other was Prince Carl Gustav Bernadotte, nephew to the Swedish King. Erickson persuaded Bernadotte to wine and dine high-ranking Germans in Sweden – a neutral country in obvious danger of invasion – to smooth his perilous mission.

Erickson persuaded the Germans he was a Nazi then went on a guided tour of their oil fields

Right: **Admiral Wilhelm Canaris was among the most high-ranking Germans to assist the Allied cause.**

Above: **Captain Eric Erickson and his wife leaving London's Surrey Commercial Docks aboard the liner *Ostrobotina* bound for Sweden.**

Erickson put his superb memory into overdrive and took details of refineries and production plants home in his head. Once in Sweden, he committed the information to tape and sent it to American agents.

There was a backlash from his friends and relations and continued pressure from the Gestapo who remained suspicious of his American birthright. Nevertheless, Erickson managed to continue his tours of Germany and the occupied territories and dispatched the information he gathered to the Allies.

He recruited a network of agents and acted as a courier for at least one other Allied agent operating behind enemy lines, a svelte brunette named Marianne von Mollendorf. It was not long before Eric and Marianne became lovers.

By May 1944, German oil production was shattered by the Allied bombardments. Now there was no oil left for Erickson to purchase on his 'buying trips' so he concocted a story about building a synthetic fuel plant back in Sweden to aid the Nazis.

At the end of 1944 when he flew to Germany he was picked up by members of the SS and taken to the notorious Moabat jail. Believing the game was up, Erickson prepared himself for the worst. Then it became clear he was a privileged visitor there to watch some executions. He was not going to be killed – but to his horror he realised one of the victims was to be his lover Marianne.

LOVER SHOT

Barely more than a glance passed between the two intimate friends before a burst of machine gun fire ended her young life. Erickson knew that if he betrayed any emotion he too would be shot. So he kept the agonising grief he felt behind a facade of normality.

He embarked on another tour, this time with Himmler's personal blessing. By this time the atmosphere in Germany had become extremely tense. Erickson knew he was being tailed by the Gestapo. And, if that wasn't bad enough, he ran into an old acquaintance by the name of Franz Schroeder, himself a Nazi supporter who remembered Erickson as an enthusiastic anti-Fascist. It was a desperate situation that required a desperate remedy.

Erickson thought he was being put in prison, but he was only being invited to witness an execution

Erickson threw off his Gestapo tail and followed Schroeder by taxi. As the German picked up a public payphone to confide his suspicions in an SS friend, Erickson produced a pocket knife and lunged at the back of his head. The super spy had now turned killer, a ghastly task made easier with the thought of beautiful, dead Marianne still fresh in his mind.

It was the last trip he made to Germany. Another was deemed too dangerous. But he had carried out his dual role brilliantly.

It wasn't until a month after the end of the war that Eric Erikson was revealed as a man of great courage. Still ostracised by his friends in Stockholm, the American ambassador smoothed Erikson's way back into society by holding a grand party with Erickson, his wife and Prince Carl as guests of honour. It was time to tell the truth about Erickson, the Nazi-lover who never was. At last he was received as a hero.

Ib Riis was recruited by the Germans as an agent when he lived in Denmark. When Britain occupied his native Iceland, he was sent back there to monitor troop movements. When his best friend in Denmark was murdered by the Nazis, Riis knew he

LIES

One of Churchill's famous quotes during the war was:

'In wartime, truth is so precious that she should always be attended by a bodyguard of lies.'

Below: Prince Carl Bernadotte of Sweden appeared a Nazi sympathiser when he socialised with the Germans. In fact, he was a vital cover for a Swedish spy.

must make different plans for the sake of the whole of Europe.

He was delivered to Iceland on 6 April 1942 by U-boat and went straight to the Allies to offer himself as a double agent. It was treacherous work. One whiff of suspicion would have brought about his death. But with the British convinced of his sincerity, his dual role began.

Codenamed 'Edda' by the Germans and 'Cobweb' by the British, Riis fed duff information to the Germans from Reykjavik. His greatest coup was to persuade the Germans that 250,000 Allied troops were poised to invade Norway, as a consequence of which two German armoured divisions were sent there, miles away from Normandy where the genuine invasion took place a few weeks later. His ruse involved the construction of dummy airfields and training camps in Iceland.

Riis survived the war but remained bitter about his heroism being 'forgotten' by the British.

GLAMOROUS SPY

It might have been a dangerous game but spying was not without glamour in World War II thanks to Canadian financier William Stevenson.

Stevenson became the head of British Security Co-ordination – an organisation established in New York before America had joined the war to link up with US secret services. This was a delicate operation in what was at the time a neutral country. Stevenson was given the appropriate codename 'Intrepid'.

Stevenson's information gatherers included the English playwright and wit Noel Coward

Among many famous personalities from the world of show business who were members of his espionage ring was actor Leslie Howard, who was apparently on a mission for Stevenson when his plane was shot down over the Bay of Biscay in 1941 while returning from Spain.

Noel Coward, the playwright, wit and raconteur, also gathered information where he could and passed it on to Stevenson. It was years before he admitted his role as spy.

Above: **From his US base, William Stevenson recruited many famous names from the world of show business to aid the Allied war effort.**

Left: **Debonair Leslie Howard, star of *Gone With The Wind,* worked for British Security Co-ordination before his death in a plane crash in 1941.**

GRETA GARBO

Greta Garbo, the screen goddess, manipulated contacts in her native Sweden from her home in Hollywood to keep the Allies up to date with important news and gossip.

Among other stars who played key roles in the secret war was David Niven, the suave British leading actor who became a commander in the Phantom Reconnaissance Regiment.

He disguised himself as a German officer and put his admirable grasp of the German language to good use, to provide a distration while his men got to work on sabotage missions.

Jacques Cousteau, the diver who became famous for his fascinating underwater photography, took film of a different kind during the war. Apparently a casual diver, he took to the Mediterranean waters and snapped Italian military posts on behalf of the Allies which helped in their invasion plans.

One of the most glamorous of all the spies from Stevenson's stable in action during the war was Amy Elizabeth Thorpe, an American beauty who married a British diplomat by the name of Arthur Pack. A dull man, he nevertheless won postings in glamorous locations like Chile, Spain and Poland. It was there in 1937 that she

One of the most glamorous spies in Stevenson's stable was Amy Elizabeth Thorpe

Above: **Playwright and wit Noel Coward, pictured broadcasting for the BBC, secretly gathered information on behalf of William Stevenson, a.k.a. 'Intrepid'.**

was recruited as a spy by the British with the codename 'Cynthia'.

She shamelessly used her stunning looks and figure to woo important people and discovered their secrets between the sheets.

Her affair with an official at the Polish Foreign Ministry helped to elicit vital information about the development of the German Enigma cipher machine.

In 1941, when she was in New York, she courted Admiral Alberto Lais, Mussolini's naval attache, to learn Italian secret codes.

Then she moved on to the French embassy in order to crack their ciphers. France, once the ally of Britain was now part occupied and part ruled by a puppet government. The ambassador's press officer was Captain Charles Brousse with whom Cynthia fell in love. Together they rifled the embassy's secrets although they never found the cypher coding.

'Cynthia' shamelessly used her stunning looks and figure to discover important secrets

So, posing as illicit lovers, they persuaded a nightwatchman to let them use the embassy at night for a tryst. They offered the nightwatchman champagne which he gleefully accepted. It was drugged – and soon he slept like a baby. Meanwhile, Cynthia was showing an expert locksmith to the safe door and he was followed by a team who copied the secrets they found inside.

'TREASURE'

After the war, Cynthia married Brousse and they lived happily together in the south of France until her death from cancer in 1963.

She was not the only provocative agent at work during the war. Double agent Lily Sergueiev, codenamed 'Treasure', prompted MI5 to employ its first women spy master, Gisella Ashley. 'Treasure', a Russian by birth who would only co-operate with the security services if her pet poodle was allowed to travel with her everywhere she went, was regarded as a

Right: **Screen goddess Greta Garbo used contacts in her native Sweden to discover information for the Allied cause.**
Below: **Screen actor David Niven was an idol before he turned hero. He was one of many Hollywood stars to join the forces and even posed as a German in undercover operations.**

'man-eater'. MI5 bosses feared for the innocence of any young male officer assigned to her case.

ODETTE SAMSOM

Odette Samsom was another woman who was placed at the sharp end of intelligence work by the Special Operations Executive. At thirty years old, she was a mother of three, French-born but married to an Englishman who was now fighting overseas for his country.

Willing to offer her services as a translator to the British, she was taken aback when they asked her to go on active service underground in her native France. However, full of anxiety about her mother and family in occupied France, she underwent the training course and was ultimately sent to Cannes in October 1942.

There she met Peter Churchill, the man liaising between London and the local resistance movements who was destined to become her second husband. She was a courier employed on desperately dangerous missions. Had she been stopped in southern France, which was at the time swarming with German soldiers, carrying such deeply incriminating evidence, she would have been shot.

When the Germans began closing in on the Cannes network, Odette and Peter fled to the safety of the mountains in Haute-Savoie, which was considered to be resistance territory. Then her knife-edge existence of carrying communications between key members of the resistance movement began again.

BETRAYAL

It was all destined to end with her arrest and incarceration in Ravensbruck concentration camp after her group was betrayed to the Germans by an infiltrator. Although sick and subject to torture, Odette remained remarkably self-possessed during captivity. She explained later that she survived the long hours of solitary confinement because she had been blind for three and half years when she was a young girl. It made her unafraid of the dark. She was finally released by the Americans in 1945.

Below: **Sea-life photographer Jacques Cousteau secretly snapped vital Italian waterside installations and relayed his pictures to the Allies.**

SINGAPORE

A courageous commando unit made up of British and Australians sabotaged Japanese shipping in Singapore harbour until it was wiped out in 1944.

The men were taken to Singapore aboard a submarine and hid out on the Riouw archipelago in Indonesia from where they hoped to carry out their mission in 'Sleeping Beauties', or midget submarines. However, when they were spotted by local policemen, they were forced to scuttle their craft for fear the new technology would fall into enemy hands. Nevertheless, they continued their mission by paddling canoes into Singapore harbour and fixing mines to anchored cargo ships.

Relentlessly, the Japanese army hunted them down. Out of the 23-man squad, 10 were captured, beheaded and their heads impaled on spikes in the Singapore streets. Two bit on cyanide pills when they were cornered. The rest died fighting, taking many enemy soldiers to the grave in the process. The mission, branded 'a failure' despite the bravery and achievements of those involved, was kept secret for years after the end of the conflict. A campaign has returned most of the victims to graves in a war cemetery where they have been re-interred with full military honours.

Odette was unafraid of the dark because she had been blind for over three years as a child

Another woman spy who used her considerable talents for guile against the Germans was not so fortunate. Violette Szabo, the daughter of an English father and a French mother who was brought up in south London, did not return from the war.

Bold Violette was 18 years old at the outbreak of war and worked on the perfumery counter of a store in Brixton, south London. It was there following the fall of France that she met a handsome officer of the French Foreign Legion in a park.

Left: **After the war, William Stevenson recounted his role as spymaster in a book.** *Below:* **In 1947 Odette Samsom, spy and concentration camp survivor, married another British undercover worker, Captain Peter Morland Churchill.**

VIOLETTE SZABO

Good-looking Etienne Szabo, from Marseilles, was devoted to the liberation of his homeland. He had already fought in Norway, suffering frostbite and demoralising defeat, before meeting Violette. There was a whirlwind courtship in London before Etienne was moved to Aldershot. Thereafter, they wrote daily to one another, expressing their flourishing love. Soon they were wed in a service

EYE WITNESS

One British soldier who slipped through the fingers of the Germans after the round-up at Dunkirk stayed on the run in France until liberation came four years later in 1944.

'Len Arlington, one of those left behind following the evacuation, was being marched into captivity by German soldiers when he dived unseen into a ditch and emerged hours later when the files of dejected British men and their victorious Wehrmacht guards had disappeared.

It was the beginning of an adventure without parallel during the treacherous years of occupation when he was at risk of betrayal from all but the most loyal Resistance workers.

The man who grew up in a London orphanage used his Cockney common-sense to keep his freedom despite the fat rewards offered by the Germans to anyone who would give him up. Dressed as a French labourer, he once cycled past a parade of German soldiers being inspected by a high ranking officer – who made his troops stand back and saluted as the runaway went past.

On another occasion, the house where he was hiding was raided by the Gestapo. Alerted by the sound of jackboots, he escaped by the skin of his teeth by clambering through a skylight, crawling along a rooftop and then ducking past the soldiers, running barefoot to a friend's house some two miles distant.

Len proved an immense asset to the Resistance by being able to spot Nazi impostors attempting to break up escape rings organised for Allied airmen. He fell in love with Marcelle Faucomprez, the daughter of a family which sheltered him, and finally married her in 1946. Len's incredible story is told in the book 'The Man the Nazis Couldn't Catch' by John Laffin.'

Above: **Peter Churchill was a hero of the French Resistance and the Allied spy network after his astonishing survival in enemy territory during the war.**

at a register office that was interrupted by an air raid.

There was a brief, ecstatic honey-moon before Etienne was dispatched by sea to fight in East Africa. Following the successful campaign, he returned to Liverpool for just one week to be reunited with Violette before flying to Cairo.

When their daughter Tania was born, Etienne was holed up in the Western Desert under pressure from Rommel's army. Soon after, in the opening rounds of the Battle of El Alamein, he was fatally wounded.

It was weeks before Violette heard of his death. She was devastated for herself and for her baby who would now never know her courageous, handsome father. Yet Violette quickly found comfort after receiving a mysterious letter. Her talent for speaking French had been noted in her records when she worked for a while with the ATS. Now she was recruited as an agent to work behind enemy lines with the expanding French resistance.

STEN GUN FIRE

On her second mission behind enemy lines in the run up to D-Day Violette was captured after a shoot-out with German soldiers. She had pinned down a number of troops with fire from her sten gun allowing another Frenchman with her to escape.

She was taken to Fresnes – a prison outside Paris – to be interrogated, then on to the Gestapo headquarters in Paris itself to face torture. She nevertheless refused to comply with the demands of the German officers to spill the beans on her fellow agents and their aims.

Violette was interrogated and tortured at Gestapo headquarters at Fresnes prison outside Paris

As the liberating forces approached Paris, Violette and other prisoners were transferred by train to Ravensbruck concentration camp. From there Violette was alternately sent to work outside the camp or detained in punishment blocks.

SHOT IN THE HEAD

When the war ended there was no news of her for months. Finally, a Ravensbruck camp commander confessed Violette and two other British women had been shot in January 1945. They were dispatched with a bullet to the back of the head, their thin, battered bodies still bearing the marks of torture, then incinerated in the camp crematorium. Violette was posthumously awarded the George Cross and the Croix de Guerre for her courage.

Below: **Violette Szabo sought revenge on the Nazis when she joined British intelligence. Her exploits as a commando won her medals for her courage, posthumously given after the war.**

PARTISAN RESISTANCE

'Whatever happens, the flame of French resistance must not be quenched and will not be quenched.' Those were the fiery words of Charles de Gaulle on 18 June 1940 in a BBC broadcast to his countrymen.

A little known French tank commander who fled to London when Hitler's forces overran France in 1940, Charles de Gaulle was to become the leader of a resistance movement which mushroomed over France.

Wherever Hitler's armies stormed in, a covert opposition would inevitably spring up. And as the extremes of Nazi behaviour became increasingly evident, sympathy towards and membership of resistance groups would flourish. Consequently, France, Belgium, Holland, Denmark, Norway, Greece, Yugoslavia and Czechoslovakia all had resistance movements, some of which were larger and naturally more successful than others.

Their role was to harry the Germans, sabotage their operations behind the lines, keep London informed of German army activity and assist escaped prisoners or crashed airmen to safety. Following the D-Day landings, the members of the resistance movements in Europe fought alongside the Allies to rid their countries of the Nazi menace once and for all.

Local people would go hungry while German officers sated themselves at the best restaurants

If the resistance groups burgeoned, then German troops had no one but themselves to blame.

As invaders, they took the best of everything for themselves, including food, accommodation and transport. Often local people would go hungry while German officers ate fine food at the best local restaurants. Prices escalated and decent clothing and footwear became outrageously expensive and out of reach to the ordinary folk of the region.

Opposite: **German retribution against suspected Partisans was swift. The sight of a local woman or man hanged in the street as a warning to others in the occupied territories was common.**
Above: **A Moroccan freedom fighter wearing a steel helmet taken from a dead soldier prepares for night patrol.**
Left: **The weapons used by Partisans were often outdated. Their main advantage lay in local knowledge.**

◆ EYE WITNESS ◆

N.I. Slugachov fled a German train containing thousands of Soviet prisoners as it crossed Poland and went on to lead a partisan group.

‘We started with small operations, concentrating mainly on hunting down agents provocateurs and Nazi spies and were the assault groups, as it were, of a party organisation.

A Pole of German origin whom the Nazis employed as an informer lived in the village of Srednie Lany. We marked him down for execution. We went to his house at night, tied him up and made him give us the names of the Nazi informers in the neighbouring villages and also of the people he had betrayed. After that we took him to the house of the elder, called the villagers together, read out the death sentence and carried it out on the spot. To safeguard the villagers against trouble, I left behind a note which read: ‘This is what will happen to anybody who works for the Germans.’

At another time we went to a village in broad daylight and found the tax-collector there. He had with him a vice and iron tags which he hung in the ears of the pigs, calves and cows, thus marking them as German property which the peasants could neither sell nor slaughter. Our men called the villagers and in their presence hung the tags on the ears of the Nazi minion, giving the people a good laugh.

Then there was the raid made on the cashier's office at a railway station in front of the noses of the police and German gendarmerie. Our men got away with money that the party needed for organisational expenses.

Word of our operations spread through the region. We had the support of most of the population who invariably coloured up the truth about our operations and exaggerated our strength and armaments. The Gestapo and the police combed the villages and forests but could never find our trail.’

Furthermore, the German troops violated the personal liberty of those in the countries they occupied. Night curfews curtailed free movement and there were frequent identity checks, often at gunpoint.

Perhaps the biggest burden that was placed on the occupied peoples was the introduction of forced labour by the Germans. This would tear men and boys from their homes and loved ones. They were shipped off to Germany to work on undermanned farms or in factories, where they frequently had to face the hazards of Allied bombing raids, while the rest of the family was left to manage as best it could.

The introduction of forced labour tore men and boys away from their homes and loved ones

Thousands of young men went into hiding. They found a welcome in the ranks of the newly formed underground armies intent on disrupting Germany's grand plan. When America entered the war, it seemed to many in Europe that Hitler's days were numbered and they were encouraged more than ever before to fight back in any way possible.

GUERRILLAS

Of course, it was no soft option being part of a resistance group. The penalty on discovery was death. Not only resistance members but also their families and comrades were put in grave danger.

The activities of such groups often brought disaster down on the heads of many fellow countrymen. From 1941 it was common practice for the Germans to shoot 100 civilians in reprisal for the killing of every German officer.

While captured airmen or troops were protected by international law, no such umbrella existed for guerrilla fighters. The most gruesome tortures were earmarked for captured members of the underground in a bid

Left: **Those captured by the Germans and found guilty of assisting the Allies had little hope of survival.**

Right: **General de Gaulle, here shaking hands with Free French Army General Leclerc, was the Resistance figurehead.** ***Below:*** **The Resistance was a family affair with sons helping fathers dismantle pavements to build barricades in Paris.**

to extract valuable information. Death almost always followed. Still, no amount of terror could quell the nationalist fire burning in the bosom of Europe's oppressed peoples.

No terror could quell the nationalistic fervour in the bosom of Europe's oppressed peoples

One of the largest and most active resistance movements was in France. France had been divided after its conquest in 1940, and the resistance operated both in the nominally independent Vichy France and in the fully occupied territories. The outlawed group became known as the Maquis, a Corsican bandit word meaning brushland.

Figurehead of the movement was Charles de Gaulle. However, it was hero Jean Moulin who unified the different strands of the movement by forming a National Resistance Council (CNR). He was betrayed and murdered by the Gestapo in 1943.

FRENCH MAQUIS

The vast open areas of France, including mountains and forests, gave the Maquis plenty of scope for hiding itself away from the Germans to carry out its brief of causing havoc behind enemy lines.

Yet there were still more members of the resistance who lived normal lives in towns, rubbing shoulders every day with the hated Germans.

Most trusted cells of the resistance were in regular contact with Britain through MI9, an organisation cloaked in secrecy that had been set up specially to help stranded Allied servicemen out of hostile terrain. The

◆ EYE WITNESS ◆

Bill Crowell, from Nova Scotia, Canada, joined the army in the summer of 1943 and arrived in England aged 19 for the battle of Normandy.

‘I was a private at the lead of our battalion one morning coming into a little village when a German jumped out of the ditch at me. I nearly pulled the trigger of my gun until I realised he had his hands up. He was surrendering. He was blubbering, terrified and couldn't really talk. It was my job to march him back as a prisoner of war.

I had been in trouble for being separated from my group before so I decided to take him only a little way. Some French people came out of their houses and lined the street, staring at us. A young French man with a commando knife leapt towards me, making for the German. He was going to slit his throat. When I gestured to him with my bayonet he threatened to slit my throat. I went ahead and left the German with some officers.

Back with my unit, we stopped at a crossroads and my corporal sent me down to the left to check for Germans. I came to another crossroads when I suddenly heard a shot being fired by my head. I crouched down and looked around. There was another shot. Behind me came three Frenchman including the one with a knife who I had seen earlier that day. Now he was carrying a sten gun. They signalled that there were some Germans in a farmhouse ahead. These Germans shoved an old lady outside the door so we couldn't shoot at them.

The Germans circled the house, crossed a small bridge behind it over a river and then blew up the bridge. One of the Germans popped up from behind a bush and waved to us before running off.

The Frenchman who had been so fierce lifted his lapel and showed me a pin bearing the cross of Lorraine, the symbol of the French underground. He took it off and gave it to me. He wanted someting in return but I had nothing to give him. I went back to my platoon soon afterwards but I never forgot the Maquis. So on the 50th anniversary of D-Day I took a plaque to the same spot where I spoke with him that day dedicated to the ‘unknown Maquis‘.’

US had a resistance aid group called MIS-X that was similar to MI9.

Transmitting coded messages by radio maintained contact with London. As Germany's technology in detecting the source of unauthorised radio messages improved, this became increasingly risky. As often as possible, a heavily coded reply was broadcast on the BBC radio network.

For the members of the resistance, there was much organisational work to do, and messages between units were of paramount importance. Couriers were at constant risk from lightning German body searches which could lead to capture and jeopardise planned operations.

Secret messages were wrapped around needles which were then hidden in cigarette casings

A favoured method of carrying information was to write down a short message and wrap it around a needle until it could be inserted into a cigarette casing. Not only was it cleverly hidden, it could be ‘smoked’ if the agents thought themselves in danger of discovery.

The French and Belgian resistance movements were crucial in helping crashed Allied airmen to escape from the occupying Germans. As there was a worrying shortage of pilots and trained air crew at one stage of the war, their actions were invaluable to both the Royal Air Force and, later, to the USAAF.

AVOIDING CAPTURE

To avoid capture, airmen who crashed badly needed civilian clothes in the local style to replace their tell-tale flying suits. It was also essential for them to put all their military training behind them if they came under the scrutiny of German soldiers and slouch instead of march, conceal their valuables and become

Left: **Gangs of anti-fascist fighters had none of the discipline or skill of regular troops but were consistently enthusiastic in their bid to rout the Germans.**

effectively indistinguishable from the local population.

Local people who were not members of the resistance were happy to help, in spite of the dangers. As the war progressed, the resistance became practised at spiriting airmen and sometimes escaped prisoners or key political figures out of danger. To locate local resistance groups, those evading the Nazis would first make contact with the local monastery or convent or the village priest.

SAFE HOUSES

The resistance could supply forged documents and all the necessary contacts from a safe house to transport and accommodation the length of southern Europe. While some fled to England straight across the Channel, most chose the safer, if considerably longer route, which took them via British-held Gibraltar.

Before assisting anyone, the resistance members would have to be convinced they had a genuine ally on their hands and not a German infiltrator. So there were a series of rigorous questions before the procedure of escape got underway.

Then the escapee would be coached in where to go, what to do and how to stay incognito.

The Resistance had to make sure the people they were helping were not German infiltrators

One of the most well-used escape routes was the so-called Comet Line which ran across the Pyrenees into Spain. This was run by a young Belgian women called Andree de Jongh. Thanks to her team's efforts, more than 700 men reached freedom.

A different route, the Pat line, was masterminded by another Belgian, Albert Guerisse, who also enjoyed a high success rate. Both de Jongh and Guerisse ended up in concentration camps for their courageous efforts, although happily neither perished before liberation came.

Before D-Day, the Allies air-dropped supplies of arms to the Maquis so that, when the time came, they could at last fight openly against the Germans.

PARTISANS

One ambitious resistance group gathered a force of 3,000 and seized the Vercors plateau of southern France. Their mistake was choosing a site far from the front line which was impossible to hold long enough for the Allies to provide relief.

A substantial German force crushed the resistance despite aid dropped by the Allies. This demonstrated that the Maquis worked better as an underground organisation than as a fighting army.

Partisan groups soon got to work in Greece and Yugoslavia. The island

Above: **Russian guerrilla fighters pore over a map and plan the best way to hit back at the superior forces of the German invaders.**

EYE WITNESS

As he travelled through France after D-Day, the BBC's Robin Duff told listeners in Britain of the bravery of the Maquis.

‘In his report, filed on 11 July 1944, he said: 'Yesterday they [the soldiers of the Resistance] were at work rooting out the Germans themselves. They were searching a deserted farmhouse when one of them saw a boot sticking out of a corner of an attic. They fired through the floor and 19 German soldiers, fully armed, surrendered to four soldiers of the Resistance.

As you stand in their headquarters and talk to them, to men who have just come back from the Maquis, to boys who are so young that they have only just been allowed to join the movement, you begin to realise something of what this movement really means. You understand why they all ask the same question: "When are we going to be called up for the regular army?"

They all say the same thing. They want everyone to know of their gratitude to the armies that have liberated them but they want still more to show that Frenchmen are ready and able to take their full part in the fight. Their chief summed it up: "Il y a encore des bons francais en France." "There are still good Frenchmen in France."’

LORRAINE

One of Churchill's famous quotes during the war included:

'The heaviest cross I have had to bear during this war is de Gaulle's Cross of Lorraine.' (Reflecting the tensions felt between himself and the leader of the Free French.)

of Crete, from which Allied forces were compelled to make a hasty departure, was full of rabidly anti-German people who were only too happy to take up arms against them.

Yet Crete was occupied by German paratroopers who deeply resented

Crete was full of people who were only to happy to take up arms against the German invaders

the losses they had suffered during the taking of the island, when many of them had been shot as they descended to earth. They recalled the ninth of their mentor Karl Student's 'Ten Commandments': 'Against a regular enemy, fight with chivalry but give no quarter to guerrillas.'

Local people were also suspected of mutilating the bodies of German soldiers during the invasion. If this happened at all, it was on a tiny scale. Yet rumours of it spread like wildfire and the Germans eagerly sought revenge. Between the May invasion and September 1941, no fewer than 1,135 Cretans were killed.

It was against this background of savagery that the highly independent village and townsfolk organised a resistance which would show no mercy to German soldiers. Mountain villages quickly became no-go zones for Germans who were already quite reasonably afraid of walking at night through the streets of Heraklion and the other fortified towns of Crete.

DEFENCE OF CRETE

It was only thanks to the enthusiasm of the local people for the Allied forces – which remained despite the debacle which had taken place in defence of Crete – that so many British, Australian and New Zealand servicemen survive the German occupation after being left stranded following the hasty evacuation.

There were so many stragglers from the forces that the submarine HMS Thrasher arrived on the island's south coast to remove as many fugitives as possible.

On Crete Britain's Special Operations Executive installed personnel to help organise the local fighters. One of them, Captain Guy Turrall, cut a curious figure as he insisted on wearing his British uniform complete with medals while trying to identify underground cells.

In Yugoslavia the most professional partisans were formed under the leadership of Josip Broz, otherwise known as Tito. A committed communist who fought with the Red Army in the Russian Civil War, he won the admiration of the Allies in his handling of the unwieldy collection of factions in his sphere.

By 1943 they were so convinced of his ability that the Allies awarded him official recognition at the expense of the Chetniks, a Serbian guerrilla group operating in the region. Embittered by this apparent betrayal, the Chetniks then began to co-operate with the Germans in a confusing volte-face. However, America's Office of Strategic Services remained in contact with the Chetniks even after they had made their own separate peace with Germany in 1943.

Below: **Marshal Tito, pictured here signing the proclamation of Yugoslavia's independence, emerged among the most successful of underground leaders.**

Left: **Hitler shows his ally Mussolini the lucky escape he had after the assassination attempt at Rastenburg.**

Yugoslavia, with its mountains, hidden valleys and extensive coastline, gave ample opportunity for the SOE to smuggle in supplies.

Partisans were so troublesome to the occupying Germans that in May 1943 some 100,000 German troops were committed to fighting the resistance movements in the region.

CROAT PARTISANS

Matters in Yugoslavia were further complicated by the activities of Croats who were pro-German and formed their own partisan groups which operated in support of the Axis powers.

On the Eastern front, anti-Nazi partisans were vehement in their opposition to German soldiers and exacted a terrible revenge for the barbarity of the Nazi invasion. Amply sheltered by the rocks, forests and mountains of western Russia, the partisans indulged less in the finer points of resistance and more in violent struggle. Their actions, often desperate and reckless, tied up German forces for days and weeks at a time, causing havoc behind the lines when the Wehrmacht was at its most stretched at the front. If they were caught, these fighters were usually hanged publicly as a warning to others.

Resistance in Germany was on a much smaller scale. This is not at all surprising, given the barbarity of the Nazi regime. The Catholic Bavarian White Rose group – one of the main resistance movements within the Fatherland itself – was wiped out almost as soon as it formed in 1943.

There was, however, still a core of anti-Nazis who continually tried to undermine Hitler's rule, both before and during the war. They received woefully little support from the British and the Americans.

The German dissident movements routed their appeals for assistance through various neutral countries, including Sweden, Spain and Portugal. Indeed, although a shot was never fired in Lisbon, the Portuguese capital was a hotbed of intrigue involving all shades of subversives. Among them was the highly educated and eloquent Lufthansa lawyer Otto John, whose job took him out of the Third Reich regularly on business. His appeals for aid were made to MI6 in Lisbon through the English novelist Graham Greene, then a counter-intelligence officer in charge of operations in Portugal.

Alas, Greene was subordinate to Kim Philby, who had already been recruited as a Soviet spy. Philby blocked all communications from the rebel Germans to the Allies. This was in accordance with his instructions from Moscow – Stalin hoped to see the Third Reich torn apart before peace broke out, and so if Germany remained intact, his plans for postwar empire-building might never have got off the ground.

STAUFFENBERG

So when the most tangible of resistance moves against Hitler occurred, with the bomb plot of 1944, the conspirators were isolated from the Allies and had to rely on their own wits in their daring attempt to pull off the assassination.

The plotters wanted to eliminate Göring and Himmler at the same time, and it was this overambition that ultimately caused them to fail. Behind the plot were Oberst Klaus Schenk von Stauffenberg, recently promoted to colonel and chief of staff General Fromm, the commander in chief of the Home Army. Stauffenberg was frequently called in to report to Hitler about finding fresh reserves of men for the Eastern Front. In league with him were Generals Friedrich Olbricht and Ludwig Beck.

The Portuguese capital was a hotbed of intrigue involving all shades of subversives

◆ EYE WITNESS ◆

Liepke Scheepstra, from Amersfoort, was a leading member of the Dutch resistance movement, called the LKP (de Landelijk Knok Ploegen). He recalls his feelings on D-day.

'I heard about the D-Day invasion by radio – we followed all reports while moving around on foot. We were glad it had happened but we hardly had time to think about the landing. We were preparing a raid on a house guarding prisoners in Arnhem and it required every bit of our energy. There was a lot at stake – people were threatened with execution. We had already attempted to free them three times but had had no success so time was of the essence.

On 11 June, we finally carried out the raid. There were seven men and a woman called 'Little Peter'. We had guns although no idea if they worked so it came down to being smart and using the element of surprise.

It was a success and 53 people came out with us. One of the first things they asked was whether the English had arrived. As I waited in the cell corridors making sure that everyone got out, a woman asked me if she could look at freedom. I took her to the door and said: 'Go on, have a sniff at it'.'

On 20 July Stauffenberg set off to see Hitler at Rastenburg in East Prussia with a bomb hidden inside his briefcase. Here was the 'Wolf's Lair', Hitler's bunker and alternative capital to Berlin.

At a high-level meeting in a reinforced hut, Stauffenberg placed the bomb as near to Hitler as he could before making his excuses and leaving. Assuming that Hitler would soon be dead, Stauffenberg made off in a car along a cobbled road through dense woods and bluffed his way past an aerodrome guard to board a Heinkel bomber for the three-hour journey back to Berlin.

Afterwards, Goebbels wrote: 'The assassination attempt was surrounded by the most dramatic circumstances and one can only repeat yet again that it is a miracle that the Führer was not maimed.'

Now the nuts and bolts of the plot which should have held it together snapped under pressure. Stauffenberg had instructed a sympathetic General to sever all communications from Rastenburg following the explosion. But lines remained open and news that Hitler was still alive winged its way to Berlin even while Stauffenberg was making his escape.

Goebbels wrote: 'One can only repeat that it is a miracle that the Führer was not maimed'

Right: **The judiciary showed no mercy to those found guilty of trying to kill Hitler. They were killed after first having being strung up with piano wire.**

GESTAPO ROUND-UP

Stauffenberg bravely carried a bomb to Hitler's Berchtesgaden headquarters on 11 July 1944 but decided against detonating it when Himmler failed to attend the meeting as scheduled. Four days later Stauffenberg attended another conference, again armed with a bomb. But Hitler abruptly left while Stauffenberg was on the phone to his co-conspirators.

Tension rose as the Gestapo rounded up suspected traitors, targeting members of the illicit group.

Alas, a fellow officer inadvertently moved the briefcase again. At 12.42, when the bomb exploded, Hitler was screened by a stout wooden table. His hair was set alight in the explosion and his trousers were torn to shreds – but he was very much alive.

Following the blast, Keitel gathered the prone body of the stunned Führer into his arms. When he realised Hitler was still alive, he wept for joy.

A German army major had been sent to arrest Goebbels but Hitler was able to personally countermand the order.

Stauffenberg soon came under suspicion and was shot with other

Above: **Partisans enjoyed some spectacular successes. The Germans who fell into their hands were either kept captive, handed to the Allies or killed.**
Right: **German officers mingled with the crowds to witness the hanging of a convicted partisan in Minsk.**

leading lights in the plot shortly after midnight. The grisly work of the firing squad was lit by car headlights. Before he died, the noble Colonel shouted: 'Long live holy Germany'.

PIANO WIRE

A further 4,980 people also paid the ultimate price for the Stauffenberg conspiracy as Hitler called for savage wholesale reprisals. Other suspects were hanged by piano wire, their final agony being filmed for Hitler's delectation. It was a reel he loved to show to high ranking German military officers to illustrate the price of treachery to the Führer.

Whole families were wiped out or carted off to concentration camps. Franz-Ludwig Graf Stauffenberg was six when his father's ill-fated bomb plot occurred. He recalls the events which followed: 'The day after the bomb my mother gathered us together and said: "Something terrible has happened – Papi is dead."

'I did not cry. Then we were told by a maid that my mother and great uncle had been taken away. Two days later my grandmother and her sister disappeared.

'Two men came to take charge of the house. I had never heard the word Gestapo before. They took us for a walk. There were six Stauffenberg children, the four of us and two cousins.

'We went to the village Catholic priest. He told us we were in bad trouble. We should always be proud of our father, he said, and gave us a blessing.'

The children were sent to a kindergarten with the children of other executed conspirators. Franz-Ludwig was finally reunited with his mother who had been kept alive as a possible

◆ EYE WITNESS ◆

Special Operations Executive agent Edward Howe parachuted into the Majevican hills to join Yugoslavian partisans.

The Majevica hideout was tucked away high in the hills. The entire region was Moslem in religion and culture. The house I was in was comparatively clean and tidy but it contained little furniture. It was used as a headquarters by the Partisans and, as I entered, I met the Partisan leaders, about a dozen of them, all seated in a circle on the floor. Everyone was eager to hear the latest news from 'outside'.

From the moment their questions began I realised how well informed they were. They listened to the BBC from London and to the Free Yugoslav station that operated 'somewhere in Russia'. I could tell them little they did not already know.

While we talked, the British planes went on dropping their loads. For the Partisans this was a great occasion. They had been starved of supplies because of their inaccessbilitiy and constant harrassment by the Germans. This unfortunate state of affairs was to continue.

The Partisans had become most efficient at sorting out supplies dropped in the darkness. It was not an easy job for sometimes chutes were blown far from the target. Everything depended on the pilot. Under good conditions, with the moon to light the area and no strong winds, there was always a chance that the supplies would fall plumb on the fires.

On the ground the Partisans would stand and watch the planes come in. Usually the pilot flashed his signal lamp to indicate that the drop was beginning and then the Partisans counted the chutes as they opened out and teams were sent off to follow each one to the ground and bring the container to an assembly point.

Here they were sorted out and stacked in piles ready to be distributed at first daylight. The practice was to have everything completed and the dropping area cleared before the day was old enough for German aircraft to come nosing inquisitively around.

Each plane – and that night five planes dropped to our pinpoint brought as many as 40 containers and other packages. Supplies of boots, for example, were 'free drops'; they were made up in bulky parcels that fell without a chute and were extremely dangerous to everyone below.

All the chutes were collected and the local people often made clothes of the silk. It was a common sight to see peasant women in that part of Bosnia wearing bright red and blue blouses made from parachute silk. Clever seamstresses also made excellent underwear for the men. In many ways this silk and the linen chutes sometimes used for stores were as valuable to the Partisan as the stores.

After what seemed a long time the sound of aircraft overhead ceased. The last plane had 'shot us up' as the RAF used to say of the final dive they made over the target. It was their way of saying goodnight and goodbye.

hostage in Ravensbruck concentration camp in August 1945.

Had the Stauffenberg bomb plot succeeded, countless Allied and German lives would have been saved and the obscene work of the extermination camps would have come to a quicker end. Despite its failure, however, the enormous pride that Franz-Ludwig still takes in his father's actions is perfectly apparent. He echoes the very sentiments of his father when he says: 'Success, killing Hitler, was not that important. It was necessary to show our people and the world that there was another, an honourable, Germany.'

The Führer decided to exterminate root and branch the generals who were opposed to him

Goebbels recorded the bomb plot and its aftermath faithfully in his diaries and by doing so revealed that Hitler still maintained the core of his following even though the war was going badly:

'The Führer is exceptionally fed up with the generals, particularly the general staff. He is absolutely determined to make a bloody example of them and to exterminate this lodge of freemasons who have always been hostile to us and have simply waited for the moment where they could in the most critical hour of the Reich stab us in the back.

BLANKET POWERS

'... I asked the Führer in the future to give me blanket powers to command the guards battalion and the Führer agrees. The consequences of the plot will certainly be far-reaching.

'At first a cleansing has to take place and the Führer has decided to exterminate root and branch the whole clan of generals who were opposed to us and in this way to destroy the wall that had artifically been built by them between army and Party and people.

'... I will take charge of the State apparatus, wielding an iron hand to restore clear lines of command.

'What does cause me to have grave doubts is the fact that the Führer has got very old. Because of the pain he is suffering, he seems fragile. Yet his being is highlighted by exceptional goodness and I have never seen him exude such inner warmth than during these days.

'One simply has to love him. He is the greatest historical genius alive in our time and with him we will either gain victory or with him we will go under as heroes.'

In the far east, the villagers of Burma and other territories conquered by Japan were little worried about the occupation. It made no difference to them whether the

Left: French Resistance workers not only had the Germans to contend with. Vichy's internal police force, the Milice, also rounded up freedom fighters. *Below:* A band of Italian partisans, including a priest, a doctor, an engineer and a 13-year-old boy, await orders. Their leader is the brother of a man hanged by Germans.

Brave men and women passed information about Japanese military activity to the Allies

foreign forces on their land were Japanese or British so there was precious little by way of a resistance movement. But there were a troop of brave men and women in the far east who risked everything to provide details of Japanese soldier and ship movement to the Allies.

COAST WATCHERS

These were the coast watchers, civilian volunteers working for Australian naval intelligence who secreted themselves around the Pacific Islands to spy on the Japanese.

Coastwatchers had first been recruited in 1919 from traders who made their homes on these islands. Now they were overrun by Emperor Hirohito's men, but they had long since established the perfect cover from which to watch out for seaborne threats mounted against the Australian mainland.

The penalty for their actions was instant death at the hands of the brutal Japanese. Yet the information they gathered gave the Allies a jump start in their battles in the region.

ENIGMA CODES

Every day, Wehrmacht commanders in the field sent reports back to base. Their dispatches included details as mundane as the weather – and as crucial as troop movements, battle plans and supply shortages. Items like these were for the ears of Germany's top brass only.

Little did the operators realise as they punched out the reports on their portable transmitters that the Allies were eavesdropping each and every time. They were also monitoring U-boats and Luftwaffe aircraft.

Early in the war, Britain cracked the secret codes which the Germans used to communicate. It was a coup which they put to excellent use as the conflict progressed. For their part, the Germans maintained an unflinching faith in the ciphers they had so painstakingly developed and stayed blissfully unaware of the enormous security breach until years after the end of the war.

Of course, Britain's code-crackers did not win the war on their own. The information they gathered was used in conjunction with other intelligence from agents and diplomats as well as the forces in the field, sea and air. But their breakthrough saved lives and helped Churchill and the other Allied leaders plan a strategy that could only lead to victory. Only in 1972 was the secret of Ultra unveiled to an astonished world.

ENIGMA ON SALE

Germany made use of a machine that had been specially developed to send encoded messages. The first model appeared in 1919 in Holland where it was designed. Soon after, a German modified the original and named it the Enigma. At the time it was a commercially available machine that was on open sale in Britain.

While tension mounted in Europe throughout the Thirties, Enigma was brought into use by the German army, navy and finally the air force in addition to the security services and the railways.

Modern warfare had rendered the telephone unreliable. As German units surged forward in their 'Blitzkrieg', they went beyond the most outlying telephone cables and risked being out of touch with their command. Also, telephone lines were subject to bomb blasts or enemy sabotage. Radio was the favoured method of communication but messages could not be broadcast in everyday language. A coding machine was necessary and Enigma was it.

Messages could not be broadcast in everyday language; a coding machine was needed

Now the Enigma was a far cry from the basic model unveiled at the end of the Great War. The Germans prided themselves on a series of advances which would keep their secrets safe.

An Enigma machine, powered by an electric battery, had similar dimensions to a typewriter and also had a keyboard. But for each letter entered on the regular keyboard, another would appear on a second, rear keyboard that would duly become the coded message. The transposition was done by three or more wheels behind the keys whose role was to scramble each word automatically. Each wheel had a multitude of settings and the code was varied from day to day.

It was a two-man operation: as one man turned the report into code, the second took a note of the new set of letters appearing in code on the

Opposite: **At Pearl Harbour the backbone of the US Pacific Fleet was smashed. When the US cracked Japanese codes, surprise attacks like this were eliminated.** ***Right:*** **Code crackers use the latest machinery in pursuit of the correct keys.**

rear keyboard and transmitted it, either by Morse code or by wireless. A machine which transmitted simultaneously and would require just one operator never came into use.

DAILY CHANGES

In theory, only the receiver of the message had the correct formula to turn the gobbledegook back into good sense. He knew the setting of the sender's machine, the correct order of the wheels and could vary his to the corresponding setting.

In its basic form alone, Enigma would have caused enough headaches for the decoders. However, there were further refinements added by the Germans as war approached. The codes were altered every day – or sometimes every eight hours – to protect its security. So one message successfully read could be followed by scores more in another, unintelligible code. Further security devices were added, too, including the coupling of letters through pairs of plugs.

The mathematical difficulties of resolving the code were mind-boggling. For their success, the British owed a debt of gratitude to Poland and its security services.

The Poles had been reading German military messages for years before the advent of Enigma. By 1929 they had acquired a German Enigma machine and within four years made huge strides in understanding its workings and output.

The Poles in turn had the French to thank for their achievements.

When documents detailing the workings of the Enigma fell into French hands via a German traitor, they were duly passed on to the Poles who put them to good use.

Although the French never cracked the German codes, the Poles were regularly translating messages generated by the Third Reich. These made alarming reading. Hitler's expansionist intentions were clear for all to see.

Hitler's expansionism was abundantly apparent to those eavesdropping behind the scenes

To help in the task of deciphering, the Poles had invented a machine they called a 'bomba' which automatically crunched codes until it hit on the right one. This was later modified and developed by the British and

Below: **The three cogs of the Enigma machine were a vital security bar. Although it looked like a typewriter, Enigma had two keyboards to create its codes.**

operated around the country by the women of the WRENS who waited patiently for results. It could take them a few moments, a few hours or even days. Then again, sometimes they failed completely to make any sort of translation.

BLETCHLEY PARK

In 1938, the Poles lost their advantage when the Germans introduced yet another complex Enigma safety system. By the time the invasion of Poland loomed in 1939, they were hopelessly at sea with the new codes.

Wisely the Poles saw a brick wall ahead of them and decided to salvage what they could of their labours. In July 1939 they met with counterparts from Britain and France and shared their knowledge of Enigma. The Poles went so far as to present each of their allies with an Enigma machine.

Although Poland was subsequently conquered, refugee decryptologists worked with the French until France too was overrun by Germany. A handful of Polish code crackers were snared by the Germans in France. Despite harsh conditions of captivity, they never once imparted the vital information about the Allied knowledge of the Enigma which would have prompted Germany to change its method of coding.

It is a tribute to all those involved that the work carried out at Bletchley Park remained secret

Now it was the responsibility of Britain alone to capitalise on the knowledge so arduously gained by their Polish and latterly by their French allies.

The Codes and Ciphers School was based at Bletchley Park, a rambling mansion in Buckinghamshire that dated back some 50 years. Gathered here were fluent German speakers, outstanding mathematicians, radio experts, military tacticians and chess players.

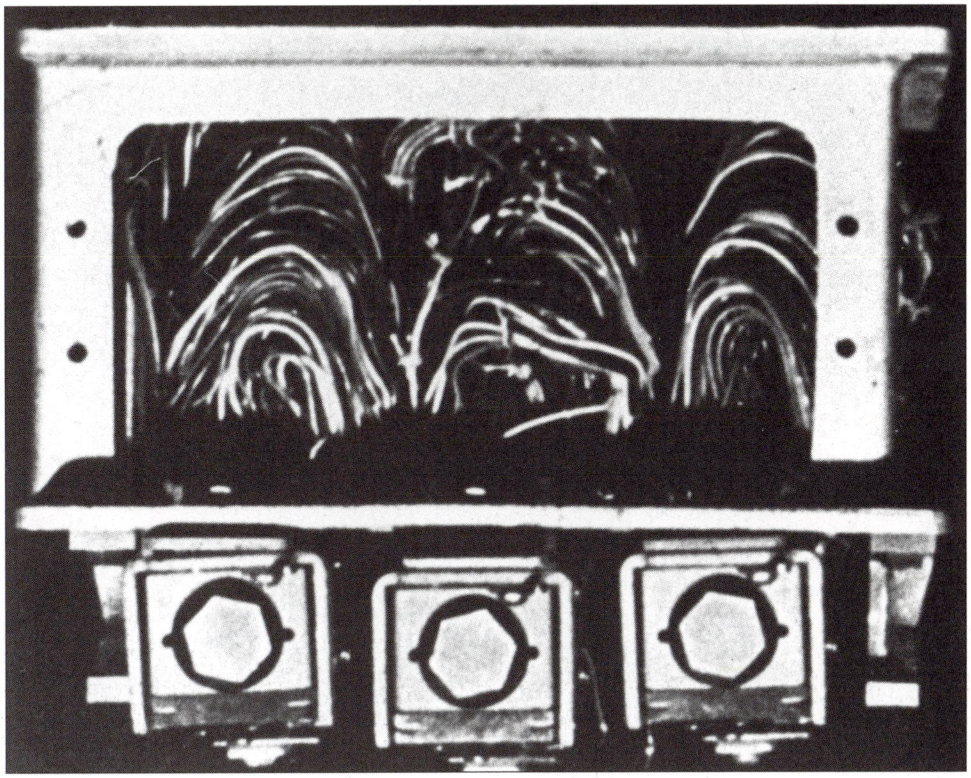

Above: **The machine used by the Americans to decipher 'Purple', the Japanese navy code.**

Some came through the services, others were plucked from universities and colleges. Their shared aim was to listen in to the German secrets and relay the information as speedily as possible to Allied commanders to give them the upper hand in battle.

Secondly, it was their avowed duty to keep their activities cloaked in secrecy. A whisper about the project could have alerted the Germans and silenced Enigma forever. It is a tribute to all those involved that the valuable work carried out at Bletchley Park remained a closely guarded secret throughout the war.

The name given to information wrung from Enigma by the Allies was Ultra. Vitally important messages were called Top Secret Ultra.

Still, the task of reading the codes was a mighty one. First came the problems in transmission. Broadcasts made over radio or wireless sets were often fogged by atmospheric conditions, leaving the eavesdropper short of chunks of the message. The installation of intercept stations to improve reception was made a priority.

Then there were difficulties in identifying the senders of various broadcasts and in differentiating between normal radio traffic and coded Enigma messages. Directional Finding or D/F was instrumental in pinpointing the locations.

British intelligence chiefs found that verbatim transcripts were not the only useful items to be gleaned from the work being done at Bletchley Park. For example, a surprise increase in the weight of traffic and a change in its locality indicated the likelihood of a fresh offensive.

To break the code itself, there was only one thing the listeners could be

◆ EYE WITNESS ◆

Earle Demone, of Halifax, Nova Scotia, served aboard HMCS Assinboine. Missions included patrolling waters off the French coast shortly after D-Day when there was concern that senior German officers might try to escape the Allied net by sea.

"One night about 9.30pm our captain comes on the radio telling us not to get undressed or into our hammocks because we would be at action stations around 1am. They obviously had some good intelligence because around 1am we sighted five armed trawlers trying to sneak out of a small port.

We were part of a patrol of four destroyers and of course we opened up on them. Two of our ships rammed two of theirs and we had all of them ablaze. Yet they still kept firing back at us. We were amazed. We couldn't understand how anyone could have stayed on those boats, never mind continue the fight.

In the end we sank four of the five. The people aboard could have got to safety if they'd wanted because they were so close to the shore. We had no way of knowing how many of them made it, nor did we ever find out the nature of their mission."

sure about: Enigma never mirrored a letter in its transposition. So for example if the letter 'a' appeared in the encoded message, it certainly would not appear in that position in the translation. That left just 25 options per letter.

However, there were short cuts which the cryptographers looked out for. Many messages contained a weather report. By matching words likely to appear in that report, they could stumble on the key to the code if they were lucky.

Sometimes messages sent in a different cypher already known at Bletchley Park were translated onto the Enigma, thus providing eaves-droppers with a welcome clue.

GLARING SIGNALS

Also, German operators became slack through over-confidence and inadvertently gave themselves away. Instead of choosing a random three-letter security code, they picked the same letters day in, day out, with the result that the listeners were then able to translate them with considerable ease. Every piece of information that was translated was kept stored at Bletchley Park for assessment by intelligence chiefs. Even the most innocent of messages was probed to see if it held a deeper meaning. As the

Even the most innocent of messages was probed to see if it held a deeper meaning

skill in cracking the Enigma Code increased, so too did the volume of associated paperwork.

The first code to be broken by the listening ear at Bletchley Park was that used by the German Wehrkreise, Hitler's home command. It was labelled 'Green' and provided little by way of hard information.

Then at the time of the invasion of Norway in 1940 the British cracked the Enigma code used by the Supreme

Below: **Work at Bletchley Park, where vital German codes were read, was kept strictly secret. Only in 1972 did its story emerge.**

Command of the German Armed Forces, called 'Yellow'. For the first time the potential of Ultra was realised with operational details being read in Britain soon after they passed between German commanders. Although the translation of Yellow was by no means complete, it gave intelligence at Bletchley Park plenty to go on and masses of encouragement.

Next to be decoded were the Luftwaffe Enigma codes, branded 'Red'. Thereafter a handle on all German air force messages was maintained throughout the war.

Gradually, the extent to which codes were broken and the speed at which German messages were translated substantially improved. By 1944 the advantage of the system was beyond doubt.

A signal containing bombing schedules for the following day sent by German High Command at 21.40 hours on 26 October 1944 was transcribed and relayed to the relevant commanders soon after midnight. Hundreds of thousands such messages were dispatched from Bletchley Park during the war. The value of the insight they gave to Allied commanders was immeasurable.

***Above:* The rear of the Enigma machine revealed some of the refinements added by the Germans after its inception in the 1920s.**

Next to be cracked at Bletchley Park were the German Luftwaffe's Enigma codes

By January 1941 Ultra gave clear indications about the German build-up for the invasion of Yugoslavia and Greece. There was little the British could do to prevent the attack, nor could it find sufficient troops to fend off the Germans. While the reading of codes failed to assist the Allies in Greece and Crete, it did help prompt the evacuation of troops. In the same year the Italian codes which dealt with shipping in the Mediterranean were cracked. This meant that the Allies could target Rommel's supply ships with ease and it substantially decreased the speed with which the German commander could progress in North Africa.

NEW U-BOAT CODES

By the end of January 1942, Bletchley Park was decrypting the naval Enigma virtually simultaneously. Convoys were routed away from wolf packs and the anti-submarine squads were able to target their prey. Ultra is believed to have saved one and a half million tons of shipping, equivalent to 350 vessels, that year alone.

U-boats were temporarily withdrawn from the Atlantic at the close of 1942. When they returned they were communicating with a new and different code which Bletchley Park could not recognise. By now Germany had realised that U-boats were the ace in their naval pack and production had been stepped up to replace those sunk by the Allies and provide more besides.

Only when the new Enigma key was broken in March 1943 were the convoy routes offered adequate protection again. Ultra coupled with improved radar, high frequency direction finding and more powerful forces, enabled the Allies to take the offensive against U-boats with a vengeance. The previously secret German refuelling points were sunk and they could now be attacked even while they were on their way towards the busy shipping lanes of the North Atlantic Ocean.

Both the Allied victory in North Africa and their success against the

Above: **Thanks to wartime code breakers, the first electronic digital computer was made in 1946.** ***Right:*** **Aircrews were saved by advance warnings from code readers.**

U-boats were key factors in the final outcome of the war. Had Rommel triumphed in Africa it would have cost the Allies dearly in terms of a vastly extended campaign. Britain, meanwhile, could have found itself besieged on the home front had the U-boats done their worst. At the very least, 'Overlord', the invasion which finally liberated Europe, would have been delayed.

The invasions of both Sicily and France were significantly assisted by the knowledge gleaned from Ultra. The decrypting of codes enabled the Allies to determine the exact whereabouts of German troops, their battle formations, the effect that air-strikes were having and all their weaknesses and strengths.

GEHEIMSCHREIBER

Not all Enigma codes were broken. While the Luftwaffe key remained in the hands of the Allies virtually throughout the war, both the army and navy keys were harder to penetrate and the Gestapo code was never read even though it remained unchanged between 1939 and 1945.

Churchill knew that Ultra was a precious gift, not to be given away lightly. It complicated issues for him and his commanders because they were unwilling to advertise its existence. Therefore, extensive use of the information gleaned from Ultra was pretty well prohibited. Only the choicest items were utilised in order that no pattern was established in the use of such high-grade intelligence. Had the Germans suspected that their codes were being widely read, they would naturally have changed them immediately.

Churchill knew that Ultra was a precious gift, not to be given away lightly

In fact, the Germans already had the Geheimschreiber, an alternative machine to Enigma used only at the highest level, which was never cracked by the decoders at Bletchley Park. There was widespread alarm that the Germans would use this for all communications, bringing Ultra to an end once and for all. Fortunately for the Allies, they never did nor did they realise the extent to which their code system had been infiltrated.

COVENTRY RAID

It led to accusations years after the war that Churchill had known in advance about the devastating air raid planned for Coventry in November 1940 and done nothing to stop it. Certainly, British intelligence did know that a city other than London was being targeted in a raid the Germans codenamed 'Moonlight Sonata', and they believed it to be either Birmingham or Coventry.

British scientists had been working on bending navigation beams used by the Luftwaffe to guide them to their targets, and thus lead them astray. On the night of 'Moonlight Sonata', 14 November, the procedure failed.

It was a clear night. This aided the German pilots, while the defensive fighter planes and barrage balloons this time claimed only one casualty between them. In a single night's work German bombers caused the deaths of 568 civilians. A further 863 were injured and the city of Coventry was gutted.

Germany, of course, listened to British and Allied messages where it could. One of its major success stories was the reading of the cipher used by the US military attache in Cairo which let them into untold secrets about British troop movements in the desert.

By 1940, B-Dienst was reading up to half of the British Royal Navy's communications

By 1940 the Führer's observation service B-Dienst was reading about 50% of Royal Navy communications, a situation that persisted until 1943 when new codes at last began to be used. This was another major contribution to turning the tide of the U-boat war in the Allies' favour.

BATTLE OF MIDWAY

Nevertheless, on balance Britain won the radio war. Likewise, American intelligence was ahead of the Japanese. The US broke the Japanese naval code and diplomatic cipher, known as 'Purple', before the fighting began thanks to the 'Magic' organisation.

Perhaps the most telling use of the US 'listening ear' was in the Battle of Midway. Admiral Nimitz was in possession of much of the Japanese battle plan days before it began. That knowledge enabled him to place some of his fleet in the Pacific where the Japanese were least expecting to find it. The Battle of Midway has since been widely acknowledged as a turning point in the war with Japan.

Below: **Some of America's top men assembled to successfully breach the Japanese radio codes.**

PROPAGANDA WAR

As the age of Hitler dawned, Hollywood, its moguls, its movies and its glamorous stars already wielded a mighty power.

Thousands of people flocked to the pictures every week to hang on the every word of their idols and absorb every nuance of the finely-spun tales. Yet as storm clouds of war gathered over Europe, the good and the great of the film-making capital were reluctant to put their talents to use in the fight against fascism.

They were not only reflecting the isolationist fervour prevalent in America during the Thirties. There were sound financial reasons for their neutral stance in that lost revenues from box offices in Germany and Italy would have hit their pockets hard.

The first film-making company to break out of the mould was Warners with its Confessions of a Nazi Spy, made in 1939 and starring Edward G. Robinson and George Sanders. Overtly anti-Nazi, it had the popular Robinson featuring as a G-man rooting out traitors who had gone to ground in America. It even contained footage of meetings of the German-American Bund, an organisation of expatriate Germans which flourished in America's Mid-West and was avowedly pro-Hitler.

Warners had good reason for antipathy to Hitler – its German agent had been kicked to death

Warners had good reason for its antipathy to Hitler. Its German agent, Joe Kaufman, had been kicked to death in Berlin in 1936 by Nazis. Now its abhorrence of the creed received yet more justification. Several Polish projectionists were hanged in their cinemas for showing the movie.

There followed a collection of films, either overtly propagandist or morality tales following little England's brave stand in the face of overwhelming odds. Few found great favour a the box office, however.

It became the crusade of a dedicated band of Jewish and other anti-Nazi writers to keep the message alive. Fortunately, their numbers grew and began to include people of real influence in politics.

Now it would only be a matter of time before film stars and makers fully grasped the

Opposite: The Olympics in 1936 held in Germany gave Goebbels a golden chance to trumpet the Fascist cause. *Below:* A scene from the anti-Nazi film *Confessions of a Nazi Spy* starring Edward G. Robinson. *Bottom:* Greer Garson and Walter Pidgeon in *Mrs Miniver*.

medium at their disposal to aid the Allied cause.

In 1940, Charlie Chaplin – playing for the last time the little tramp figure for which he was so loved – made The Great Dictator. Chaplin played two roles – a humble Jewish barber and a Hitleresque dictator called Adenoid Hynkel, who bore a striking resemblance to one another. Needless to say, there is confusion between the two and the persecuted Jewish man ends up making an impassioned speech to a Nazi rally about freedom and the rights of man. Basic in its theme, the film was nevertheless stirring.

Hollywood helped to undermine isolationism and bring the USA into the war on Britain's side

Now the messages in the movies became bolder. From MGM came Escape in which the dashing Robert Taylor rescued his mother, played by silent movie star Alla Nazimova, from a German concentration camp followed by The Mortal Storm, which also illustrated the dangers to hearth and home of Nazism.

The same year, 1940, also saw the general release of Alfred Hitchcock's Foreign Correspondent with Joel McCrea as a spy-ring buster who in the film's finale makes an emotional appeal for stepping up the war effort in the States.

At last the stage was set with Roosevelt clearly indicating his preference for Britain and the isolationists losing credibility by the month. The key was in persuading the American public that some causes were worth fighting for and it looked as if this was beginning to filter through.

MRS MINIVER

There were a number of anti-German films before America was brought into the war, none quite as accomplished as Mrs Miniver.

Made in 1941 and starring Greer Garson and Walter Pidgeon, it was

Below: Charlie Chaplin played two roles in his satirical and poignant film _The Great Dictator_ which ridiculed both the Nazi and the Italian Fascist systems.

EYE WITNESS

Mrs Miniver, the acclaimed anti-Nazi film of 1942 which won an Oscar for Best Film, did much to sway public feeling toward the British in America. It featured the following sermon delivered by a vicar in a bombed-out church.

"This is not only a war of soldiers in uniforms. It is a war of the people – of all the people – and it must be fought not only on the battlefield but in the cities and villages, in the factories and on the farms, in the home and in the heart of every man, woman and child who loves freedom. Well, we have buried our dead but we shall not forget them. Instead they will inspire us with an unbreakable determination to free ourselves and those who come after us from the tyranny and terror that threaten to strike us down. This is the people's war. It is our war. We are the fighters. Fight it, then. Fight it with all that is in us. And may God defend the right."

an out-and-out tribute to Britain's home front which scooped a clutch of Academy Awards. Little could have done more to drive home the message. Audiences up and down America wept with Mrs Miniver over one woman's tenacity and tragedy in the conflict. They barely had time to recover when they were crying on their own account. Pearl Harbor brought America into the war at the end of 1941 with the deaths of thousands of their own servicemen.

CASABLANCA

Hollywood studios were vacated by the cream of their stars who either volunteered for military service or joined troop entertainment facilities. Among those who went were Clark Gable, James Stewart, Mickey Rooney, Tyrone Power and John Ford. British stars who donned a uniform included David Niven and Laurence Olivier.

Right: Josef Goebbels, the accomplished Nazi propagandist to whom Hitler owed much of his staying power.

Women stars sold war bonds, toured the Pacific and Europe to brighten up the lives of the troops or served refreshments in canteens.

Now the film-makers who remained behind channelled all their energies into winning the propaganda war against Hitler.

Out of this era came what is possibly one of the greatest films of all time, Casablanca. Humphrey Bogart was mean and moody while Ingrid Bergman was as delicate as a rose. The lovelorn pair forced apart by the war in Europe captivated the free world then and continue to do so even today.

Satire and parody had their place too. The swipes taken at Nazis in the enduring To Be Or Not To Be kept the audiences entertained while leaving them with the clear impression that all German men in uniform were humourless dimwits. Many came away with the impression that SS stood for Stuffed Shirt.

Apart from films with a barely hidden message, many others were made with a 'feel good' factor, escapist stories designed to keep morale high on the home front, particularly musicals.

Besides making the box office blockbusters, Hollywood's fount of talent contributed to the war effort by making documentaries and stirring series demonstrating the value of American-style democracy.

So thanks to Hollywood film, perhaps the most popular medium of the age, the message of the Allies was presented to the receptive British, American and Australian publics, who flocked to the cinema.

Masterly though Hollywood became at manipulating messages for the benefit of the Allies, it was competing with the best.

Germany had a master in its upper ranks in Josef Goebbels, who took charge of all forms of public expression when the Nazis came to power.

Born in 1897 of devoutly Catholic lower middle-class parents in the Rhineland, Josef Goebbels was psychologically inhibited in his childhood by a disfiguring club foot. In adulthood he hardly topped five feet in height and barely tipped seven stones on the scales.

Germany's master of media manipulation was Propaganda Minister Josef Goebbels

Nevertheless, he had a quick and able mind which won him a place at university. He was able to take up the opportunity thanks to financial support from a Catholic fund. The loan gave him a certain obligation to the church. But when the money ran out, so did his faith. The charity eventually sued him for the money.

at first a devotee of Gregor Strasser, a radical revolutionary who ran a branch of the party at odds with that that of Hitler. Goebbels once even demanded the expulsion from the Nazi party of 'the petit bourgeois Adolf Hitler'.

Ambition, however, moderated his extremism. He finally recognised Hitler was the man who would take the party to great heights.

Below: **Goebbels had the common touch and knew the way to the hearts of the Reich's soldiers.**

From there, Goebbels turned his hand to writing books and plays. None was successful and he blamed the 'Jewish literary mafia' for that rather than looking for his own

Goebbels was a writer who blamed his lack of success on 'the Jewish literary mafia'

shortcomings in style and ability. In 1925 he joined the Nazi party which appeared to reflect much of what he thought and felt at the time. He was

By 1928 Goebbels was the party's leader in Berlin and five years later, when Hitler came to power, he became Minister of Propaganda and Entertainment in the new Reich.

He was himself an accomplished public speaker, well able to rouse the passions of his audience with an apt quip, taunt or compliment until they were putty in his hands.

It wasn't long before this gift for assessing the public mood got to work on a larger canvas. Under his expert eye, all press articles, radio broadcasts, exhibitions, posters, feature films and news reels were given a pro-Nazi slant, often with a blatant disregard for the truth.

◆ EYE WITNESS ◆

Lance Corporal Heino Vopel was with an SS division in Normandy in 1944.

'I didn't know anything else. In 1933 when Hitler came to power I was eight years old. Then came the marching and the singing and carrying flags. That was in the youth movements. All that propaganda I only fully understood 20 years later. Everybody was taught blind obedience and knew nothing else.

If you looked up in the sky on D-Day the aircraft were like a plague of flies. Wherever anything moved, they shot it. Anything that moved, whether it was someone with a bicycle or a car or a lorry or a tank or a horse.

We had a driver from Munich in our team who was 32 and had two children. He was always saying: "This is madness – why don't we just give up? We haven't got a chance."

But we younger ones were still hopeful and we had been so influenced by propaganda since our time in the Hitler Youth that we thought we could never go under.

After D-Day I thought how am I going to get out of this mess, or should I try to desert? But I was scared because in Russia there had been a counter-offensive and that is when the Germans had found deserters. The advancing Germans shot all of them because they were deserters.

At the time I said I was fighting for Volk and Fatherland. I know now that was probably wrong but at that time I couldn't just say I didn't feel like doing anything. I had to defend my Fatherland.'

■ PRO-NAZI SLANT ■

News and entertainment programmes made by the Allies were imported then shamelessly cut to 'expose' the population as degenerate and their leaders as teetering icons.

Perhaps his greatest talent was for never allowing dogma to interfere in his work. Historians have since accused him of lacking ideals and inner substance. Certainly, he was never blinded to reality by fascist

Left: Impressive Nazi rallies helped to win the hearts and minds of ordinary German folk. *Below:* Germany produced its own films to rival those of Hollywood, subtly reinforcing the state's propaganda.

aims in the same way even as Hitler. Accordingly, he was opposed to starting the war with the West which he felt was unwinnable. This unpopular opinion cost him some standing in the party. By 1944 he was counselling Hitler to make a separate peace with Russia to save Germany from annihilation. The hated adversary could become a valued ally once more, he argued, to push back the advance from the West.

Goebbels was opposed to starting the war with the West which he felt was unwinnable

Yet this lack of restraint was in itself a strength. His ideas were always fluid, allowing him to plot a sure and certain course to success rather than be hidebound by the conventions of fascist beliefs. His gestures were always calculated and to get him what he wanted – they were never from the heart.

His personal contradictions were manifold. He dressed smartly in expensive suits and was a notorious womaniser. Yet at the same time he possessed a puritanical streak which baulked at extravagance and had him sneer at the lavish lifestyle of rival Hermann Göring. He remained aloof from other members of the Nazi hierarchy whom he regarded as little better than contemptible, swaggering beer cellar bullies.

Hitler came to rely on the faithful Goebbels to translate his unsavoury messages into a form that would be readily and eagerly devoured by the German public. Although he himself didn't invent the lies of Nazism, Goebbels certainly played a major part in propagating them. He skilfully manufactured a myth of infallibility which even survived Hitler's death. Without Goebbels in tow, it is questionable whether Hitler would have maintained his hold over the German people for a dozen years.

The relationship between the two men was never personally close, although Hitler was a witness to Goebbels' marriage to Magda in 1931. When his wife later sought divorce on account of the runtish Goebbels' string of ill-concealed love affairs, Hitler intervened to effect a reconciliation between them.

UNDER THE SPELL

Yet Goebbels and Hitler were lost in mutual admiration. Goebbels fell under the spell of Hitler's magnetic power in those early days of Nazism and never looked back. For his part, Hitler saw Goebbels as something of an intellectual who shared the same artistic aspirations. Of course, Goebbels wasn't an intellectual. He would burn books of great worth because they were written by Jews or contained left wing philosphies, along with the rest of the Nazi thugs. He did this even if he admired the content of the book, so detached was he from his inner feelings.

RABBLE-ROUSER

In fact, Goebbels steered clear of addressing himself to the great thinkers of the day on the basis that they could never be converted to Nazism if they weren't already. His work was consequently directed at the man in the street whom he saw as much more malleable.

While Hitler undoubtedly had a fascinating charisma, only a fraction of the population got to meet him personally. It was for Goebbels to project this image and recruit loyal servants throughout the Reich. His aim was to bring a radio into every German household, because that way the words of the master could be brought to all the population.

His control of cinema became a legendary example of how to sway the minds of the masses. Films containing messages contrary to the Nazi cause were banned. New films bore the Goebbels hallmark of artistic uniformity. By the time the film industry was nationalised in 1942, many of its brightest talents had quit Germany in disgust, unable to find an outlet for dissenting opinions.

Goebbels quickly realised that to hammer away at the Jews could provoke a backlash

Goebbels quickly realised that to hammer away at a theme like the hatred of Jews could provoke a backlash. So the messages in the works he liked best were subtle. Only a few films diminishing the Jewish race were produced while historical spectacles recalling the triumphs of Bismarck and Frederick the Great, containing possibly one Jewish villain, were favoured instead.

In fact, much of the output of the state-controlled industry was devoted

◆ EYE WITNESS ◆

Peter Bielenberg, a long-standing opponent of Nazism, was one of the plotters in the failed 1944 coup against Hitler. Luckier than most, he survived and was sent to Ravensbruck concentration camp.

"For my legal exam I prepared with a Jew. We both passed. But I was able to continue my career and he could not. I was outraged. When Jews were deprived of their civil rights by the Nuremberg Laws in 1935, this was not thought to be so atrocious. People had had it drummed into them that Jews were second-class citizens. Germans had been told they were awful since the last war and here was Hitler telling them they were great again. The Germans have a tendency to obey orders and just hope for the best in an unpleasant political situation."

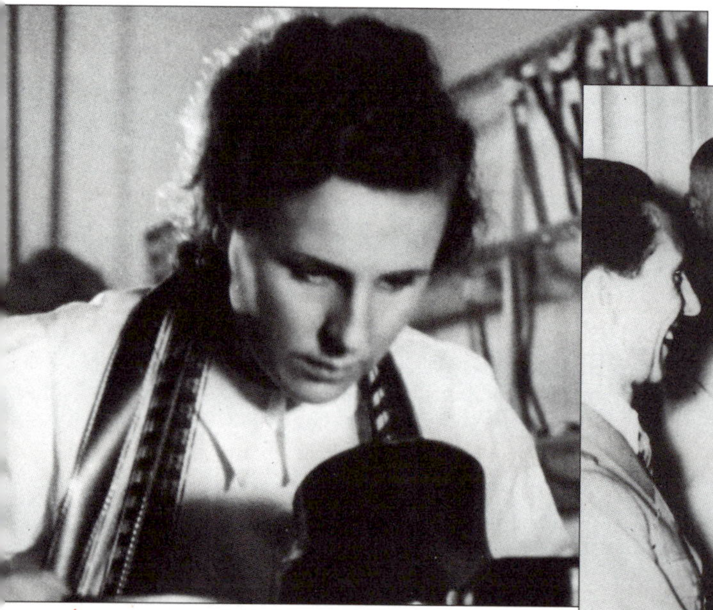

Above: **Leni Riefenstahl laboured to produce some of the most stunning propaganda films of the age.**
Right: **Her reward was the admiration and support of Hitler himself.**

Left: **From a BBC studio, J.B. Priestley and Leslie Howard rallied the listeners with pro-British broadcasts.**

to comedies and fantasy giving the German people their quota of escapist movies to relieve them of the pressures of the war.

LENI RIEFENSTAHL

The two outstanding propaganda films made in the era were Triumph of the Will, capturing the Nazi party Nuremberg Convention of 1934, and Olympia, a tribute to the 1936 Berlin Olympics. Both were made by Leni Riefenstahl, an actress and dancer turned film-maker who embarked on her new career during the ascent of Hitler in Germany.

Her copious talents won her the accolade of Hitler's favourite film-maker – and with good reason. She had an uncanny knack of promoting the Nazi cause with scarcely a mention of it by name.

He killed his wife and six children with cyanide and then took the same poison himself

Allegedly, she became a mistress to the Führer – a charge she constantly denied. Following the war, she was jailed by the French for peddling Nazi propaganda and spent nearly four years behind bars before being freed. All attempts to revive her film career failed and she worked instead as a stills photographer in magazines.

As the war continued and Germany's fortunes declined, Goebbels became increasingly extreme, his speeches more and more outrageous. It appears he began to believe the propaganda that he was distributing – that, against all odds, Germany could win the war after all. He even believed that if only he had been Chancellor the war could have ended in victory. His faith in his own talent never wavered.

On 22 March 1945 Goebbels records in his diary: 'My war propaganda is now being eulogised quite openly in London. It is being said that it is the most exemplary of all the war efforts being made anywhere today and that it is primarily responsible for the fact that German resistance is so much in evidence, even though on a reduced and enfeebled scale.'

Both he and Hitler were convinced that America would pull out of the war on the death of Roosevelt. When their gleeful prophecy proved wrong, both had to face the inevitability of defeat. After presiding over the funeral of his master Hitler in May 1945, he killed his wife and his six children, aged between four and 12, with cyanide and then poisoned himself in the besieged Berlin bunker which had become his final shelter.

In contrast, Britain's propaganda was hopelessly awry when the war broke out. It was amateurish, condescending and ineffective, and one of the first suggestions to emerge from Churchill's publicity department was the necessity to provide tea following an air raid.

Britain always shied away from the use of propaganda. Its ham-fisted attempts to blacken the name of 'the Hun' during World War I backfired when they were quickly exposed to be nothing but a pack of lies.

Now there was a reluctance to use such measures, no matter how extreme the international situation. Government advisor Horace Wilson was outraged at the suggestion by Eden in 1938 that the BBC, press and British Council should get their heads together and produce a unified output to help combat the menace

EYE WITNESS

On 1 May 1943, Goebbels made the following entry in his diary.

"The Soviets at the moment are extremely insolent and arrogant. They are quite conscious of the security of their position. They have no consideration whatever for their Anglo-Saxon allies. The men in power in the Kremlin know exactly how far they can go. There is a great bitterness in London and Washington about it which nobody seeks to disguise. The Anglo-Saxon camp is in a blue funk about the fact that our propaganda has succeeded in driving so deep a wedge into the enemy coalition."

posed by Germany. In a memorandum to Prime Minister Neville Chamberlain, Wilson wrote: 'Having been old-fashioned for very many years, I find myself unable to show enthusiasm for propaganda by this country and I still cannot bring myself to believe that it is a good substitute for calmly getting on with the business of government, including a rational foreign policy.

'... I do not believe that any propaganda is really harmless. Even if you are careful, in praising yourself, not to decry others, the unflattering implication is always there. Ten days ago, the British press acclaimed our diplomatic efforts in the cause of peace. That could be read as implying that Germany was on the point of an act of aggression. It was so read in Germany and bitterly resented. The example is worth quoting as showing how easily the most harmless publicity may give offence.'

This feeling that propaganda somehow wasn't quite cricket infected the launch of the service charged with producing information for the public. Its staff, though well meaning, had no training in the art and lacked the common touch.

Consequently, the Ministry of Information was soon publicly scorned for its inadequate efforts. Comedians like Tommy Handley and satirists like Evelyn Waugh had a field day.

GAS MASKS

There were numerous posters issued offering advice on how to put on a gas mask. Yet attack by the enemy did not come for months. The posters appeared pointless.

They were accompanied by a volley of 'do's and don'ts' from the government which even tried to close down cinemas for the duration of hostilities – until they realised the extent of the potential of film for entertainment and the dissemination of propaganda. The Ministry of Information constantly referred to the public as 'you', making ordinary people feel like underlings. The patronising tone of posters aimed at raising spirits on the home front merely succeeded in irritating people.

Above: **American Jesse Owens swept the board at the Berlin Olympics – and was promptly ignored by the Führer.** ***Left:*** **The Führer hoped the Olympics would be dominated by Aryans.**

There were hoardings galore advocating the wisdom of evacuation, showing a mother shielding her children from bombs falling from the sky. But bombs had not fallen from the sky as expected. Bureaucracy had gone mad. At this stage of the war, Hitler had done little to inconvenience the masses while the government had done a great deal.

British attempts to smear Germany during World War I had backfired when exposed as a pack of lies

Rationing itself was not resented by the majority. They were keen to see signs that the war was affecting rich and poor alike and across-the-board measures did just that.

Another weakness in the information channels quickly came to light. The service ministries were happily dispensing information to news organisations without reference to the MOI, an error which Goebbels would never have made.

DUNKIRK

As Britain's fortunes of war declined, so the MOI feared a threat to morale. It came as something of a shock following Dunkirk and the Battle of Britain to find that, in spite of the government, the populace was keeping chirpy. Still, they kept back information about the war for fear of inspiring defeatism. It was hard facts that the public desperately wanted.

The vast majority were merely frustrated by the bumbling efforts of the Ministry of Information. A stock phrase on the radio following reports of an RAF action was 'all our planes returned safely'. It was widely disbelieved and rightly so.

Above: **Humphrey Bogart and Ingrid Bergman are still best remembered today for their roles in *Casablanca*.**

As the British government's obsession with secrecy took an iron grip and few details were released about the war effort in general and troop movements in particular, people tuned in to the propaganda broadcasts made from Germany by traitor William Joyce, better known as 'Lord Haw-Haw' because of his plummy voice. After listening to his version of events and discounting the obvious German slant, British listeners at least felt they had an inkling of what was going on.

During the Blitz, the Ministry happily handed out pictures of a housewife clearing up her broken windows with the incredible caption: 'Well, there's one thing about this Blitz. It keeps you busy and you forget the war.'

While the people of London were stoical, they were far from delighted at seeing their houses blasted. Reports claimed that the air raids had made little impact – these were designed to undermine the German effort, but they inflamed the British, too. It denigrated their efforts. And later, when other British cities were flattened in bombing raids – and then they were not even mentioned on the national news – there was further justified upset.

Gradually, the officials learned that lack of information adversely effected enthusiasm for the war effort. The Germans knew exactly where they had bombed even if they didn't know the extent of the damage they had inflicted. So there was little point in suppressing the whereabouts of the latest raids.

Posters which exhorted the population to work harder when they were already doing their utmost also caused a widespread negative effect. Less derogatory and more effective were straightforward slogans like 'Dig for Victory' and 'Save Fuel for Battle', to which everyone could relate. The most useful and well-received of all posters were those used in the 'Careless Talk Costs Lives' campaign, simple in message and beautifully drawn by Fougasse, and the recipes for rationed food, even if some contained expensive ingredients not found in many working-class kitchens.

Britons tuned into broadcasts from Germany by William Joyce, better known as Lord Haw-Haw

THE TIDE TURNS

After the Allied victories in 1942, the Ministry of Information's job became much simpler. News of victory in North Africa had a far greater effect on public morale and production figures than any poster or radio message ever could.

FILMS

The top money-spinning films in the UK during the war years were:

1939: *Pygmalion;* Forerunner of the musical *My Fair Lady* in which a professor tries to turn a flower girl into a 'duchess' within six months, starring Leslie Howard and Wendy Hiller.
1940: *Convoy;* A story of sacrifice as a British merchant ship goes under to save a vital convoy. Unknowns Clive Brook and John Clements starred while the acclaimed director Pen Tennyson was later killed in action.
1941: *49th Parallel;* Eric Portman, Laurence Olivier, Leslie Howard and Raymond Massey were the stars of this drama set in Canada about five U-boat crewmen attempting to escape to the US.
1942: *The First of the Few;* Called *Spitfire* in the US, it was the story of the plane's creator R. J. Mitchell and once again starred Leslie Howard.
1943: *In Which We Serve;* A host of stars including director Noel Coward, John Mills, Richard Attenborough and Celia Johnson peppered this flag-waving epic about the survivors of a torpedoed destroyer who remember their recent pasts.
1944: *This Happy Breed;* A portrait of family life in the London suburbs between the wars, from a play by Noel Coward.
1945: *The Seventh Veil;* Polished romantic drama starring James Mason and Ann Todd about a talented concert pianist suffering from divided loyalties.

TRAITORS

Among the grey apartments of a Parisian suburb, gaunt-faced Jews were herded from their homes in terror for their lives. Sour-faced guards, quick to administer a powerful kick or stinging punch to the stragglers, knew the fate of their prisoners well enough.

These quiet, clean-living Jews were bidding a desolate final farewell to the country where they were born and bred. Stinking, airless carriages were ready to ferry them into Germany and its appalling concentration camps where sickness, starvation and death were almost inevitable.

The guards who relished the unsavoury task of committing these helpless folk to their doom were no rabid Nazis, however. They had not sworn allegiance to Hitler nor were they even German nationals.

Here were French people who enthusiastically seized the opportunity to carry out the Reich's dirty work. Without apparently turning a hair, they set about the task of ridding occupied France of its Jewish population with alacrity. Neighbours, colleagues and even friends were no longer safe, so eager were certain members of the French population to do their duty, as they saw it. Members of the French police force were joined by civilians for the effort to rid all France of Jews.

They set about the task of ridding occupied France of its Jewish population with alacrity

In every land that fell into German hands, there were a good number of collaborators who would do the Nazis' bidding. For them, the chance of power and aggrandisement from the invader was worth more than any loyalty to their own country's flag. In France the actions against the Jewish people were even sanctioned by the government who introduced two rounds of anti-Semitic laws to exclude all Jews from public life. Those people who carried out the grim work of the Nazis were traitors, no more, no less.

BLACK THURSDAY

On 16 July 1942 came Black Thursday, the biggest anti-Jewish operation since the Fall of France. In all, 12,884 people, including 4,051 children, were taken to transit camps or the notorious Drancy concentration camp in France before being transported to Germany where virtually all died.

This reflected a rich vein of anti-Semitism rife in French society even before the outbreak of World War II. The influx of Jewish refugees from Germany and, later, Poland had done nothing to abate feelings which were running high. By 1939, there were upwards of 150,000 Jews in Paris – although that figure was only a fraction of the number of foreigners

Opposite: **French Jews rounded up by neighbours bound for Drancy concentration camp.** ***Below:*** **Marshal Pétain co-operated with the invading Germans.**

EYE WITNESS

Dirk Bruggeman was 17 and en route to the German higher school in Arnhem when he heard about D-Day. His parents were members of the NSB (Nationale Socialistische Bund), a pro-Hitler group in the Netherlands. Now a priest in the Hague, he is associated with the 'Stichting Werkgroep Herkenning', the Foundation of Recognition, an organisation for children of parents with mistaken beliefs.

On the way I saw a group of people by a newspaper office where a bulletin read that the Allies had landed in the Seine Bay and I wondered how this could be possible, believing it to be in Paris.

I didn't have my uniform on that day. Strangely enough, I had mixed feelings. On the one hand, I found the news threatening, and on the other hand, exciting. Real war was getting closer.

The atmosphere at school was uneasy. The teachers remained courageous but I believe that in their hearts they were working out how to save their own skin. On the outside there was an air of: "Oh, we will contain them." For months afterwards we believed we would contain them and didn't want to believe in the destruction of our ideal.

I never doubted my father's ideals. The Nazi songs were impressive, so was the marching, and so were the special uniforms of the Hitler Youth to which I belonged. You felt exceptional and strong.

However, I was a delicate and vulnerable lad and not at all sporty. I didn't actually fit in to this showy atmosphere but I couldn't tell anybody this.

It is still a major question for me: Could I be to blame? Should I have acted differently? If I could change things then I gladly would but I understand that my fate now is to live with the past.

living there at the time. Already, the Jews were under pressure from expulsion orders and police harassment.

When the invasion came, Paul Reynaud was Prime Minister with Marshal Philippe Pétain his deputy. Pétain was a key rallying point, in Reynaud's eyes. He had won victories in the field against Germany during World War I and helped to steer France from defeat to triumph. Despite his advancing years – he was 84 years old – he was a hero figure to many French people.

Despite his great age, Marshal Pétain was a hero figure to many French people

It was Pétain who signed the armistice with Hitler that left one third of France unoccupied. He assumed control of that free state from a base at Vichy. Despite his willing subservience to the German invaders, many French people still admired Pétain as the man who delivered France from a costly and protracted war with Germany.

PIERRE LAVAL

Alongside him was so-called socialist Pierre Laval, an experienced statesman and confirmed pacifist who won the patronage of Hitler, so much so that when he was sacked by Pétain, his reinstatement was ordered by the Führer himself.

Although Pétain and Laval were far from being friends, they cooperated together to assist the

Left: **In court after the war Pierre Laval denied he was a tool of the Nazis even though he had Hitler's personal support for his actions during the Occupation.**

Germans and finally even allowed them to cross Vichy territory, destroying any illusion of independence. Ironically, neighbouring Italy – which was run by the Fascist Mussolini, an ally of Hitler's – actively provided a bolt hole for Jews forced to flee from Vichy France.

OBEYING ORDERS

Pétain, Laval and their cohorts at grass roots level denied responsiblity for what happened to the French Jews. Those in command professed ignorance of the real purpose of the deportations. Those carrying out the commands insisted that they were only doing their job.

The French branch of the Gestapo ran its own torture chambers. The Milice, Pétain's paramilitary force, used methods whose barbarity rivalled those of the SS.

Following the war, Pétain was tried as a collaborator and sentenced to death but reprieved by de Gaulle on account of his great age. He lived until 1951. Laval fled to Germany following the liberation of France but was finally persuaded to return. After a trial he received the death penalty and was executed by firing squad.

There were even rumours of a more sinister collaboration in France, that of tacit assistance given to the Germans by the Union Générale des

There were rumours of a pact between the occupying Germans and French Jews

Israelites de France. It was feared that the organisation, run by established French Jews, contributed towards the deportation schemes at the expense of poor immigrants in a bid to save the native Jewish population. After the war it was cleared by a jury of the charge not once but twice. The rumours probably arose because the unpopular UGIF allowed itself to be manipulated by the Germans and French and became responsible for tax collection and administration of aid, which was sorely lacking.

After the war the French took a terrible vengeance on Nazi collaborators during the Occupation

QUISLING

Collaborators in France were to suffer the vengeance of the Resistance. More than 9,600 were executed without trial following the liberation of France. In later trials a further 7,000 were sentenced to death, although only 767 were killed. In all, about 40,000 people received jail terms for aiding the Germans.

In Holland, there were similar sympathies for the Nazis in sectors of

EYE WITNESS

Madeleine Tomin, from Le Havre, northern France, fell in love with a German soldier and had his baby. When France was liberated, her neighbours sought revenge.

"When they came for me I thought they would break down the door. Luckily my boy, now two, was asleep. I was frog-marched into the street where men and women held me down. Their faces were twisted with hate. They were calling me *putain* (whore) and *traitre* (traitor). At least three pairs of hands pushed me down on to the pavement then somebody else grabbed a handful of my hair and started hacking away with a pair of scissors. I breathed deeply to hide my fear. But I could have choked when a razor flashed before my eyes. It was scraped across my scalp so painfully. The crowd were whooping and baying. They daubed swastikas on my forehead using mud from the gutter. I never felt more wretched before or since."

Below: **Vidkun Quisling (*centre*), the Norwegian whose name became a byword for treachery, stands under armed guard after the war.**

the population. The Nationale Socialistische Bund was formed for Nazi supporters. They donned uniforms and helpfully carried out the wishes of the invader, particularly with regard to the rounding up of Jews and communists.

Vidkun Quisling was head of the puppet government set up in Norway by the Nazis

In Norway, Vidkun Quisling actively courted the Germans even before they invaded. His name has since become a byword internationally for all traitors and fifth columnists, those who work within a country to secure its downfall.

Quisling led the National Union Party in Norway and was rewarded for his devotion to the Fatherland by being made 'minister president' of the puppet government set up there by the Germans. Arrested in 1945, he was found guilty of war crimes, having sent countless numbers to their deaths in the gas chambers of extermination camps in Germany, and executed.

RESISTANCE

The first Aryan German to be executed for showing signs of resistance died at Sachsenhausen concentration camp. He was a communist working in the Junker factory at Dachau. When he refused to carry out air raid protection work he was reported by the works police, arrested and sent to be quizzed by the Gestapo in Berlin. It was Heinrich Himmler who ordered his death, intolerant of even the most token element of resistance against the Third Reich. Even today, the name of the hero resister is unknown.

German communists continued to carry out acts of sabotage during the war. They also tried to help prisoners of war and slave labourers when they could. The best known are Bernhard Bastlein, Franz Jacob and Theodor Neubauer who set up an underground network spanning a dozen towns. All were killed by the Gestapo in the last year of the war.

Although German resistance was notoriously small-scale, Gestapo records in August 1942 reveal that 1,761 Germans were arrested for striking; 1,583 were detained for having contact with imported workers or POW's; 1,210 were held as suspected anti-Nazis and 1,007 were branded resisters.

LORD HAW-HAW

Perhaps the traitor who was best known to British people was William Joyce, otherwise known as 'Lord Haw-Haw'. Born in America of Irish parents, he was a devotee of British fascist Oswald Mosley. He arrived in Germany in 1939 on a British passport and happily broadcast propaganda for the Nazis throughout the hostilities. British families crowded around their radio sets to hear his news and views, not because they believed what he was telling them – on the contrary – but because they were starved of information about the war effort by the Ministry of Information.

Left: **William Joyce, popularly known as 'Lord Haw-Haw', broadcast pro-German propaganda to the British throughout the war. His messages were treated as comical.**

After the war, Joyce tried to escape capture by blending in with the refugees in Germany but his voice – the hallmark of his life of treachery – gave him away. He was arrested, tried for treason and executed.

Other British traitors included a motley crew of about 200 who fought for Hitler in the 'British Free Corps'. The Corps was primarily established for Nazi propaganda purposes although it did see action on the Eastern front.

Some of those in its ranks were motivated by ideology, some were on the run from British justice and others had been persuaded to change sides after being taken prisoner by the Germans. At least one corps member, Thomas Cooper, is almost certainly responsible for slaughtering many Jews in Poland. He was never brought to trial.

The Corps was founded by John Amery, son of Leo Amery, one of Prime Minister Churchill's cabinet colleagues. John Amery, declared bankrupt in 1937 aged just 24, became embroiled in politics by running guns for the Nationalists during the Spanish Civil War. Rather than return to England after the outbreak of war, he lived in France and finally moved on to Germany in 1942 where he broadcast in favour of Hitler over the English airwaves.

It was his idea to create the St George's Legion in defence of Germany and on the offence against Bolshevism. His aim was for it to fight 'with the best of Europe's youth to preserve our European civilisation and our common cultural heritage from the menace of Jewish Communism.' In the British press it was dubbed the Legion of the Damned.

Amery won initial support from the Germans but they soon became disillusioned by his erratic behaviour. He was sent back to France; his unit was renamed the British Free Corps and put under the command of New Zealander Roy Nicholas Courlander, a lance corporal who had been captured in Greece in 1941.

Two years later, Amery was heard making propaganda broadcasts on the radio. He followed those up with visits to the 'stalags' in a bid to recruit Allied prisoners of war into the Corps. Following the war, he maintained he carried out these actions under duress or as a method of undermining the Germans. It proved a weak defence.

About 200 Britons fought for Hitler in the 'British Free Corps' on the Eastern front

The value of the Corps in terms of propaganda to the Germans was two-fold. Not only could they broadcast to the folks back home in Britain and help spread confusion and doubt. But they could also be set up as examples of how woefully poor Allied soldiers really were. The men who were attracted to this form of treason were without exception weak and pitiful. Their main daily occupations would be drinking and whoring. Then, when they thought they were about to be sent to fight on the dreaded Eastern front, they manifested an appalling display of cowardice which can only have put the disciplined German soldiers in good heart.

Right: **John Amery was the son of a British cabinet minister yet still betrayed his country to the Germans in pursuit of wealth and prestige.**

HAROLD COLE

Like Joyce, John Amery was hanged. While their treachery was carried out through misguided allegiances, one man during the war was motivated mostly by the desire for self-preservation. His name was Harold Cole, a cockney who earned the title at Scotland Yard of 'the worst traitor of the war'.

Before the war he was a conman operating on the continent and at home and the subject of police dossiers in England, France and probably other countries too. He had a string of aliases and a bold and confident manner.

In 1939, aged 33, he joined the British Expeditionary Force and became a sergeant in the Royal Engineers. Following theft and illicit liaisons with local women, Cole was put under arrest but repeatedly escaped from his military guard.

Cole took the best option open to him. He deserted in Flanders and went on the run. Yet it wasn't long before the dapper Englishman was recruited into British intelligence to help downed Allied airmen escape out of France.

He carried out his perilous duties with skill, already being well-practised in the art of subterfuge. But Cole lacked the commitment necessary for such noble duties. When the Germans rumbled him, he turned traitor and delivered countless Allied escapees and French Resistance workers into the hands of the Gestapo. He even double-crossed the woman he claimed to love. All the while, he was lining his pockets with cash from both Axis and Allied spymasters.

The lifelong petty criminal had now become a murderer. Yet at the end of the war, he posed successfully as an American and helped to root out the Germans for whom he had previously worked. He somehow used his remarkable powers to evade the Allies who were keen to see him brought to justice. It wasn't until he was killed in a shoot-out with French police in a Parisian bar in 1946 that summary justice was at last dispensed.

THE V BOMB MENACE

In the early hours of 13 June 1944 a new age of weaponry dawned when four pilotless aircraft sped across the British coast and headed for the capital.

One hit Bethnal Green where it killed six and wounded nine. The others landed harmlessly. This was just the start. Two days later more than 200 were launched on London. The tally rose to more than 3,000 in the subsequent weeks.

The Germans called them Vergeltung (Retaliation) missiles or V-1s – in the hope they would be the the first in a series of secret weapons which would bring Britain to its knees. The British public knew them better as 'doodle-bugs' or 'buzz bombs'.

The Germans called them V-1s; to the British they were known as 'doodle-bugs' or 'buzz bombs'

They had been a long time coming. Allied intelligence had realised that a new breed of terror for British civilians was being nurtured in the laboratories of Nazi Germany. In fact, there were two separate projects both vying for Hitler's favours. One was the pilotless aircraft, a relative newcomer to the field of hush-hush weapons, and the other was the rocket.

Pilotless aircraft had been mooted by a leading manufacturer in Germany in 1939. Only in the aftermath of the 'Baedecker raids' mounted on British cities in reprisal for strikes against Germany in the spring of 1942 did they appear on the agenda again. For although the Luftwaffe raids caused havoc in some of Britain's historic cities, many of the bomb loads missed their targets altogether. For this disappointing result valuable men and machines were risked. A new weapon which preserved these assets would be welcomed by the Luftwaffe despite its haphazard targeting.

When three established companies put their heads together on the project, there was enough evidence to convince Field Marshal Erhard Milch that it was viable. On 19 June 1942 he ruled its development and production should be given high priority.

The first to be launched on Christmas Eve that same year travelled a mile and three quarters and was judged to have a sufficiently reliable aim.

A little behind schedule, mass production of the missiles got underway along with the installation of 96 launching sites in northern France.

The purpose of the launching sites was the subject of widespread gossip among the local French labourers employed to build them. The ski-shaped ramps and supply buildings were unorthodox shapes and clearly visible from the air, so it was only a matter of time before Britain's aerial reconnaissance detected them.

In reply, Air Marshal Arthur Harris arranged a telling strike against Peenemunde, the Baltic base which Britain had correctly identified as being at the heart of developments for Hitler's secret weapons.

PEENEMUNDE RAID

On 17 August 1943 a flight of 571 heavy bombers visited Peenemunde, bombing by moonlight from 8,000 feet, an uncomfortably treacherous height. Pathfinders who had marked the targets assisted the bomber pilots in their demanding task.

Despite smokescreen defences, bombs still ravaged the target until the arrival of German fighters who had been misled into believing the attack that night was to be on Berlin. They claimed 40 RAF bombers.

Yet although the raid cost Bomber Command dearly, it had telling

Opposite: **Barrage balloons were one of three defences against pilotless aircraft, otherwise called V-1s or flying bombs.**
Above: **Barrage balloons were unable to prevent bomb damage.**
Right: **A Typhoon aircraft pursues a V-1 over British countryside.**

Above: **A German rocket on its launch pad in northern France aimed and ready to fire at targets in London.**

consequences. The production of secret weapons was undoubtedly hindered. The subsequent delay in the development and launching of both the pilotless aircraft and the rocket was crucial. Had either been in use before 6 June 1944, the forces gathering for 'Operation Overlord', the invasion of France, would have been at risk.

General Eisenhower went as far as to say: 'It seemed likely that if the Germans had succeeded in perfecting and using these new weapons six months earlier than they did our invasion of Europe would have proved exceedingly difficult, perhaps impossible. I feel sure that if they had succeeded in using these weapons over a six months period, and particularly if they had made the Portsmouth-Southampton area one of their principal targets, "Overlord" might have been written off.'

This is probably an exaggeration but it nevertheless serves to illustrate how essential the Royal Air Force engagement at Peenemunde was to the overall conduct of the war.

By November 1943 British aerial reconnaissance experts correctly identified a midget plane measuring about 20 feet across its wings pictured on the ground at Peenemunde as a pilotless aircraft. They took this as their cue for another round of bombing raids.

ALLIED BOMBING

Between 5 December 1943 and the end of the year, the combined might of British and American air forces dropped more than 3,000 tons of bombs on the sites thought to be earmarked for the launch of secret weapons. The first fortnight of 1944 saw another 20,000 tons of bombs rain down on those designated areas. Afterwards, British experts claimed 21 of the sites had been destroyed. German records put the number at only seven.

If the Germans had had pilotless aircraft six months earlier, D-Day might not have happened

Sensing the danger, Germany's hierarchy took steps to disguise their project by rebuilding launching sites which were, in fact, obsolete, clamping down on communications into and out of the bases and spreading

Right: **Despite the shortcomings of the flying bombs, the German top brass responsible for the project were proud of their achievement.**

disinformation throughout the Resistance networks.

As D-Day approached, air chiefs were unwilling to spare aircraft for further raids. Thus the secret weapon programme was then left unharried.

Pressure was brought to bear on the German scientists, still not happy with the launching of the flying bombs, to initiate a strike against England soon after D-Day.

Confusion reigned at the launch sites as the prescribed date drew near. Although there were plenty of missiles and adequate fuel, none of the sites had its full quota of safety equipment. Thus German commanders risked substantial numbers of crewmen in order to comply with the order to start the flying bomb offensive immediately. They appealed for a postponement but they were allowed just one hour.

In the end, the expected salvo did not materialise. Only ten missiles were launched, five of which crashed at once. A sixth disappeared, probably coming down in the sea, while the remaining four reached England.

The bomb could travel at up to 400 miles per hour and as high as 3,000 feet. Inside the nose of its streamlined fuselage was packed one ton of explosive. Behind the warhead was a tank with a capacity of 150 gallons, sufficient for a journey of

The bomb could travel at 400 mph at a height of 3,000 feet; it had a range of about 130 miles

about 130 miles. For steering, it relied on a magnetic compass and a pre-set automatic pilot. It had small wings and a tail.

As its journey ended, the propulsion unit would cut out. Thereafter, it nose-dived towards the earth, silent except for the rushing sound made by a heavy object travelling at speed through the air. Its effect was usually more devastating than that of a bomb because it exploded before it hit the ground.

Vigilant members of the British Royal Observers Corps were the first to spot the bombs as they split the night air. They noted 'a swishing sound' and spotted a bright red glow firing from the rear end of the missiles.

Soon many people living in south-east England, especially residents of the so-called 'Doodlebug Alley' along the path taken from France towards London, came to recognise the sinister outline of a pilotless aircraft in the sky. And they knew from bitter experience the terror inspired at the moment the noisy motor cut out just before the bomb fell to earth.

◆ EYE WITNESS ◆

In his memoirs, armaments chief Albert Speer recalled Hitler's reaction to the V-1s.

❝Hitler and all of us hoped that this new weapon, the V-1, would sow horror, confusion and paralysis in the enemy camp. We far overestimated its effects. I myself did have some doubts because of the low speed of these flying bombs and therefore advised Hitler to launch them only when there were low lying clouds.
But he paid no attention. On 12 June, in response to Hitler's premature command, the first V-1 pilotless jets were catapulted off their launch ramps in great haste. Only ten of them could be dispatched...Hitler forgot that he himself had insisted on rushing matters and vented his fury at the bungled project upon the builders.

At the situation conference Göring hastened to shift the blame to his opponent Milch and Hitler was on the point of deciding to halt the production of the flying bomb on the grounds that it was a wasteful blunder. Then the press chief handed him some exaggerated, sensationalised reports from the London press on the effects of the V-1. Hitler's mood promptly changed. Now he demanded increased production and Göring too declared that this great achievement of his air force had always been a favourite project of his. Nothing more was said about Milch, the previous day's scapegoat.❞

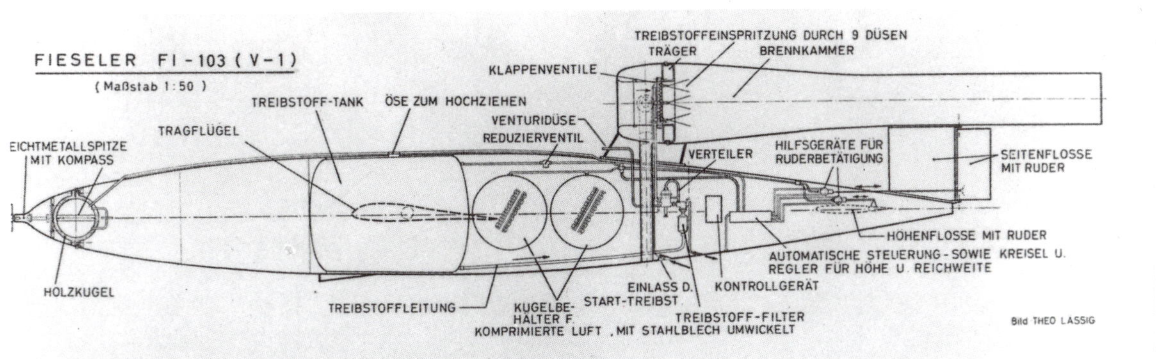

***Above:* Designer's blueprint for the V-1.**
***Left:* The ominous outline of a V-1 bomb in flight brought a chill to the hearts of the British people.**

The introduction of doodlebugs into the war brought unprecedented terror to London. People were far more frightened by a robotic weapon launched at London from some distant spot than they were of even the worst nights of the Blitz.

Within a matter of seconds, 121 were killed and a further 80 injured in the Guards Chapel

EVACUATIONS

There was a new wave of evacuations organised by the government. And for the first time citizens who endured the privations of living in London in its darkest hour dug deep into their own pockets to finance refuge for themselves in the country.

The City of London, Penge, Bermondsey, Deptford, Greenwich, Camberwell, Lewisham, Stepney, Mitcham, Croydon and Chiselhurst were among the most badly affected areas of the metropolis.

Churchill succinctly expressed the effect that the secret weapons had on the people of London:

'This new form of attack imposed upon the people of London a burden perhaps even heavier than the air raids of 1940 and 1941. Suspense and strain were more prolonged. Dawn brought no relief and cloud no comfort.

'The man going home in the evening never knew what he would find; his wife, alone all day or with the children, could not be certain of his safe return. The blind, impersonal nature of the missile made the individual on the ground feel helpless. There was little that he could do, no human enemy that he could see shot down.'

GUARDS CHAPEL

At first the new bombs caused little loss of life. But one bomb landed by fluke in central London and changed all that. On Sunday, 18 June 1944 a bomb cut out over Birdcage Walk and dived into the Guards Chapel at Wellington Barracks.

Right: A prototype of a piloted bomb given the name V-3 but never launched.
Below: When its engine cut out, this V-1 bomb descended silently upon Piccadilly in the heart of London.

DAD'S ARMY

'Dad's Army', the Home Guard formed as an auxiliary army in 1940 when Hitler was poised to invade Britain, was disbanded in November 1944. At one time it had 1,084 battalions involving 1,701,208 men and 31,824 women.

A packed congregation was in attendance that morning, among them active and retired servicemen, together with their wives and families. There were 121 killed that morning and a further 80 injured within a matter of seconds. The chapel, built in 1830 and renowned for its sumptuous interior, lay in ruins. It took three days to find the bodies under the rubble. Astonishingly, 40 worshippers were discovered alive in the debris.

Anti-aircraft guns, fighter planes and barrage balloons were all used to counter the V-1s

Winston Churchill and the king and queen visited the site while rescue work was in progress. It was a stark pointer to the power now lying in Hitler's hands.

English author H. E. Bates gave a graphic account of the devastating effect of V-1 rockets in his book Flying Bombs Over England written in 1945 when he was an Air Ministry squadron leader.

'The doodlebug could be heard from a long way off. It came out of the clear summer distance or out of the rain or the dark July cloud with a low level roar that could be heard about 30 miles away.

'[The doodlebug] seemed to fly on an invisible track as straight as a train. As it came nearer, the roar became a metallic throb like the fiery stroke of a cheap motorcycle. As it passed overhead, these throbs set up the most deafening reverberations that were like the explosion of a continuous backfire.

'And since the enemy's favourite tactics were to launch the bombs in salvoes, they rarely came singly. As many as half a dozen would come roaring over together on parallel tracks separated by about a mile.

'The noise was fantastic. People who had never been frightened by the sound of a bomb or bomber found

Right: **Flying bombs not only carried explosives but also enormous quantities of fuel to power their flight. The tell-tale exhaust was at the back.**

themselves nervous at the roar of the doodlebug. If the noise of it travelling was bad enough, its sudden silence was worse. That sudden silence meant that somewhere, sooner or later, the bomb was coming down.

'Wherever it came down, the lives of innocent and decent people would be terrorised or blown into a thousand unrecognisable pieces.'

London did not lie undefended, however. Anti-aircraft guns, fighter planes and barrage balloons were all used with varying degrees of effectiveness to counter the V-1.

◆ EYE WITNESS ◆

Muriel Kellaway was 18 when the buzz bombs began to fall on London.

I was on my way home one day when I could hear the sound of this bomb approaching behind me. You could hear the sound from miles away. Aircraft made a distinctive drone but this was different, more of a throbbing roar. Suddenly, the engine cut out. I wanted to run for cover but there was no shelter around. Also, I felt a desperate urge to be at home with my parents. I must have been the first woman to do a four minute mile as I dashed towards our house. The bomb fell about half a mile away. I could feel the earth shake as it went off but luckily it only demolished a wall and no one was hurt.

Then came the rockets. You couldn't hear those at all. I was serving in the cafe we ran off the Great West Road in West London at about 9.30 am one morning when suddenly there was an almighty explosion. A rocket flattened Packards, the car manufacturing factory, nearby. It came out of the blue, rather like many of the terrorist bombs of today. There was no warning at all. All the glass windows in the cafe shattered over people finishing their breakfasts but fortunately no one was injured at our place.

In the factory, it was a different matter. Every car in the area did a detour to take the injured to hospital. Scores of people died. There were a lot of our regular customers that we never saw again caught up in the explosion. We carried on serving dinners as usual while the rescue work went on.

People were demoralised by the V-bombs, certainly, but they put on a brave face and cheered each other up. Everyone was more sociable then. They were frightened but it didn't stop them enjoying themselves.

Above: **The giant, silent and deadly V-2 rocket is ready for launching at its target. Its speed was a breathtaking 4,000 miles per hour.**

ANTI-AIRCRAFT

At first, anti-aircraft emplacements in London were happy to open up on the flying bombs, because the operators were aided by the tell-tale flaming red exhaust. However, when they scored hits they risked bringing the explosives down into a crowded area when the bombs might otherwise have fallen in open country.

So the guns were moved to the North Downs to intercept the bombs earlier in their flight. Now the disadvantage was to the men of the Royal Air Force involved in the same task. Ground-based gunners were unwittingly firing on their own fliers as they tried to bring down the V-1s. The guns were moved once more, this time to the coast where radar facilities for tracking the bombs after they were launched worked even better than on the Downs. A gun belt was set up between Cuckmere Haven and St Margaret's Bay – this extended 10,000 yards out to sea and any Allied plane entered at its peril.

WINGTIP NUDGING

There were several different ways in which pilots could try to tackle a fast-moving flying bomb, but all of them were difficult and some were positively hazardous. There was, of course, the option of shooting down the missile. To do this, the attacking plane had to move as rapidly as possible – some were even stripped of paint to make that vital hairsbreadth difference between catching the V-1 and letting it escape to cause mayhem where it fell.

Another method sometimes employed was for the pilot to come alongside the V-1 and carefully nudge its wingtip against that of his own plane, sending the V-1 into freefall and sparking its destruction.

Perhaps the most dangerous technique of all was to fly in front of the bomb so that the manned plane's slipstream would throw the bomb out of control.

Fighter planes operated both out at sea, avoiding the gun belt, and inland.

The barrage balloon network on the outskirts of London also played an important role and netted 232 V-1 bombs during the war.

Bomber Command continued to do what it could to combat the V-1 threat and kept up attacks on launch sites in France even though Churchill refused to release aircraft for these missions if they were needed for battle operations in Normandy. In the event, attacks against the launch sites yielded disappointing results, and the main storage depots for the flying bombs in France proved much more rewarding targets.

About 8,000 V-1 bombs were launched against London, 2,400 of which reached their target

In July 1944 British bombers attacked and largely destroyed the natural caverns at St Leu d'Esserent in the Oise valley where 2,000 German bombs were stored. At about the same time, another similar storage station was reduced to ruins by American bombers.

Yet despite all these Allied efforts, it wasn't until the invasion forces overran the launching bases in the first week of September 1944 that the flying bomb campaign finally came to an end.

About 8,000 V-1 bombs were launched against London, with 1,000 crashing immediately after take-off and about 2,400 reaching their target. Civilian casualties amounted to 6,184 with 17,981 injured. Germany attempted to maintain its assault by launching V-1s from planes and from long-range sites in Holland but with little success.

But it was not quite over yet. Hitler still had the long-range rocket or V-2 with which he planned to avenge the invasion of France.

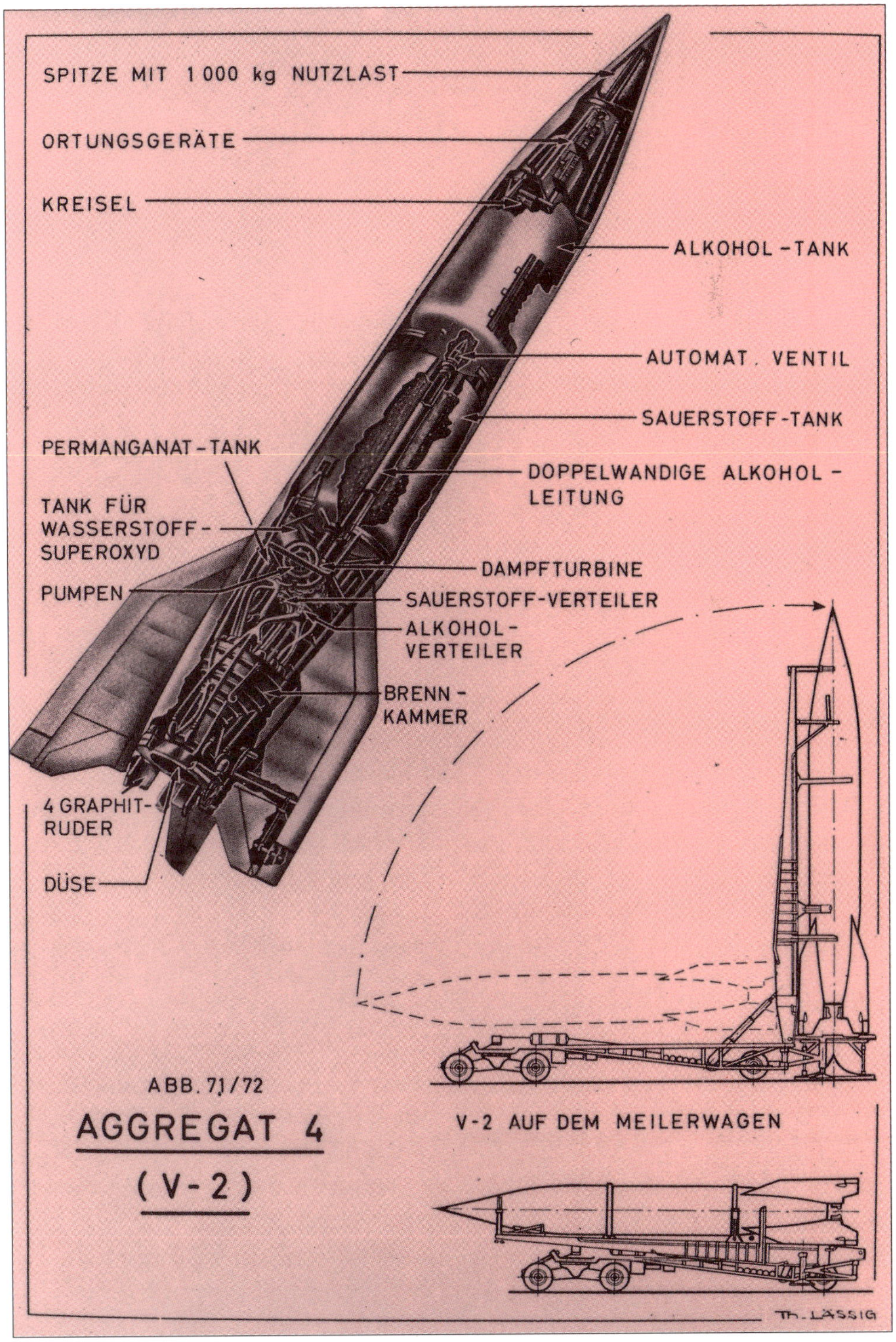

Right: **A cross-section of the V-2 rocket reveals how much of its capacity was devoted to the storage of high-octane fuel.**

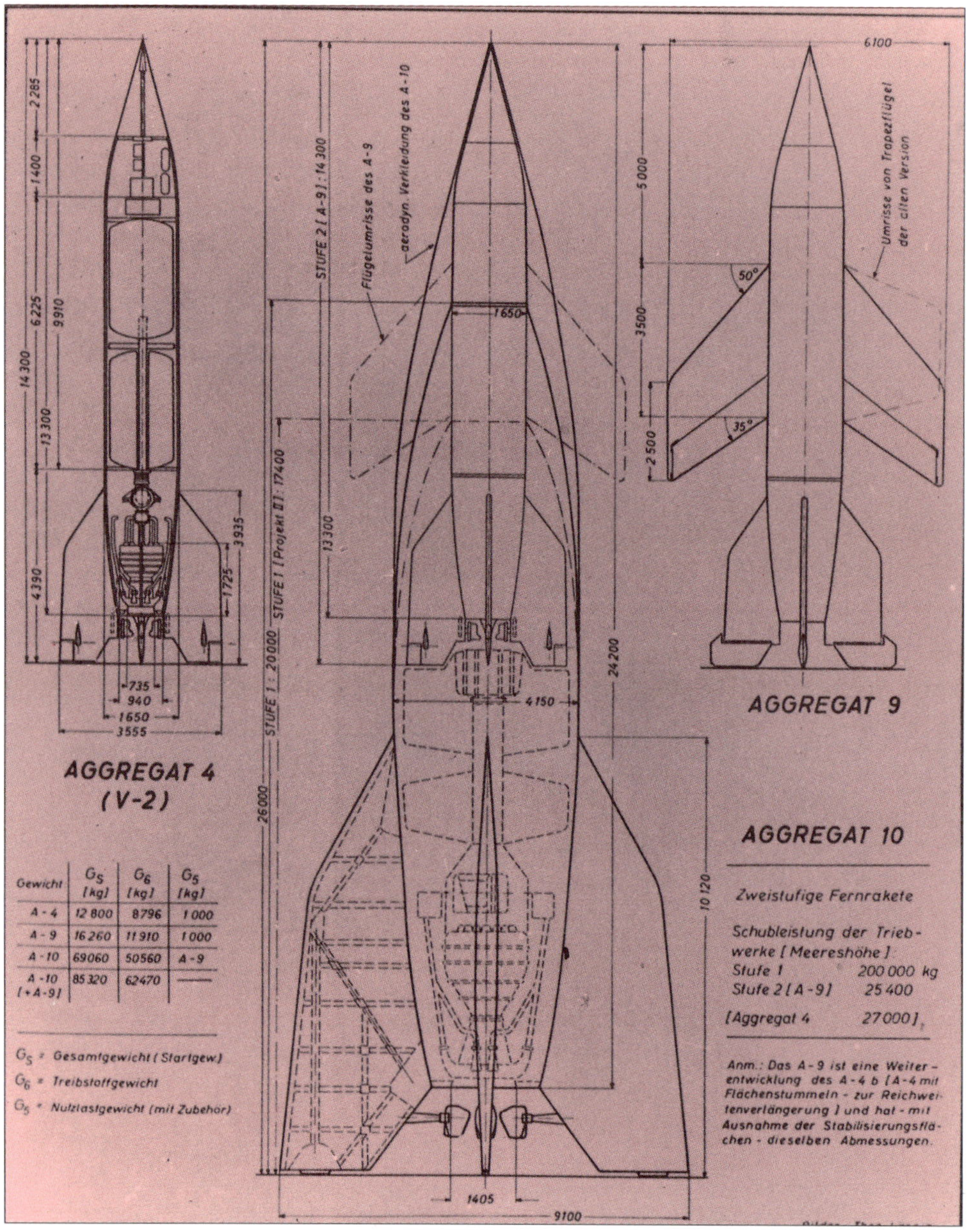

***Left:* Hitler believed his new breed of rockets would force the Allies back from the borders of the Fatherland.**

Rockets have been in existence for thousands of years. They were used as long ago as 1232 by the Chinese against marauding Mongols. By the 19th century, rockets rivalled artillery in popularity with armed forces but their technology stayed in the backwoods while that of artillery leapt ahead.

ROCKET SCIENCE

Following World War I, Germany experimented long and hard with rockets, convinced that they were working on the key weapon of the future. The major breakthrough came when scientists realised that instead of powering rockets with cumbersome and limited explosives, the answer lay in liquid fuels. It took them years to perfect their weapon, even though they were amply funded by Hitler's regime.

Rumours of a new German aerial weapon reached London in 1939 when a crowing Hitler gave a speech that all but gave the game away.

Yet scorn was poured on the idea of a rocket when a British expert, Lord Cherwell, pronounced that because it would need to weigh some 80 tons it would never get off the ground. Cherwell swayed Prime Minister Churchill and thereafter little credence was given to the dissenting views of other scientists.

The existence of rockets was slowly proved beyond doubt thanks to British intelligence. A bugged telephone conversation between two high ranking German prisoners caught them wondering why no loud explosions had been heard around their London cell when the imminent arrival of rockets had been promised while they were still in Germany.

Once again Peenemunde was the base for development. More concrete information came on 13 June 1944 when a rocket landed on Swedish soil and was shipped to Britain for further investigation.

TURBINE-DRIVEN

How had this rocket got to Sweden? The story was that a German expert in glider bombers had been invited to witness a rocket trial. So overawed was he by the sight of the rocket rising into the air that he pushed the control lever he was holding to the left and held it there, throwing the rocket well off course.

British investigators marvelled at the rocket with its jet fired by alcohol and liquid oxygen. Nearly four tons of alcohol and five tons of liquid oxygen were consumed in each minute of flight. A special thousand

Nearly four tons of alcohol and five tons of liquid oxygen were consumed each minute

horsepower pump forced the fuel into the jet chamber, which was worked by a turbine.

FUEL CUT OUT

The V-2 rose vertically for six miles and then, guided by its automatic controls, turned to an angle of 45 degrees. At the end of its range, the fuel cut out and the missile fell to earth. With a maximum speed of about 4,000 miles per hour, it took only a few minutes to reach a target anywhere in Europe.

In July, a courageous Pole was spirited to England with evidence of the rocket. Germany had pulled back its research into the heart of Poland following damaging RAF raids. Although German patrols raced to retrieve experimental rockets, one that fell was pounced on by Polish underground workers, hidden in a river until the Germans gave up their search and then dismantled by night. The Polish engineer/messenger carried technical documents and more than 100 pounds of parts to a rendezvous with an RAF Dakota on 25 July 1944. Selfless and patriotic, he returned to Poland, to be executed by the Gestapo in Warsaw on 13 August.

Little could be done to bring down the rocket once it started on its inexorable path

On 8 September the expected bomb arrived. One fell in Chiswick and within 17 seconds, another struck at Epping. Now a different bogey haunted the British people. For while there was a decent warning with the buzz bomb, there was nothing to indicate the imminence of a rocket explosion.

Above: **Dr Todt and General Olbricht were two of the leading lights in Germany's 'retaliation weapons' project. Although initial trials were disappointing, they were convinced the bombs would devastate Britain.**

H. E. Bates called it 'an ingenious and diabolical robot. It came without sound, without warning and without discrimination. Its inaccuracies were so vast that it became a weapon of monstrous chance.'

More than 1,300 were fired at London from The Hague and an estimated 500 hits were made. On average, each killed twice as many as its predecessor, the flying bomb. In all, 2,724 people were killed and a further 6,476 were injured.

Little could be done to bring down the rocket once it had started on its inexorable path. The best hope for civilians in Britain was that the Allied advance in Europe would reach the launch centres and knock them out before further damage was done.

Not only Britain was under threat. Antwerp was the target for 8,696 flying bombs and 1,610 rockets. Only recently freed from German occupation, the Belgians did not have the benefit of anti-aircraft guns and fighter aircraft to protect them.

RETALIATION

The tally of death amounted to 3,470 civilians and 682 Allied servicemen. Hitler and Göring were enthusiastic supporters of these 'retaliation weapons', certain that they would inflict immense casualties on the enemy and could reverse the fortunes of Germany. The fact that mass production of the new weapons was virtually impossible under the regular Allied bombing raids appeared to have escaped them.

Speer, meanwhile, had grave doubts. He saw cash and resources being poured into rockets and flying bombs to the detriment of other arms for the military, particularly the Luftwaffe. He declared that it took as long to produce each rocket as it would to build six or seven conventional fighters and that each one cost the same as 20 flying bombs.

Britain continued to use Mosquitoes, approximately the same price as a rocket, each of which could drop about 125 tons of bombs within a mile of its target, while a German rocket could drop only one ton of explosives with an imprecise target margin of 15 miles.

ATOMIC BREAKTHROUGH

Even before the outbreak of war, the race was on to construct an atomic bomb. It was German scientists making the running, too, as they probed the mysterious world of nuclear fission.

In January 1939 Otto Hahn and his colleagues had achieved the first stage of the process by which the weapons of tomorrow's world were made.

Eminent physicist Albert Einstein was among many to sign a letter voicing concern about the headway being made by Germany when the nation was in the hands of the mad Hitler.

Nobel prize-winning Einstein was a confirmed pacifist. But being a German-born Jew, he had refused to return to Europe following Hitler's rise to power in 1933 and knew more than most about the menace which now loomed. It was his justified fear of fascism that persuaded him to write his letter of warning to President Franklin D. Roosevelt.

'A single bomb of this type, carried by boat and exploded in a port, might very well destroy the whole port

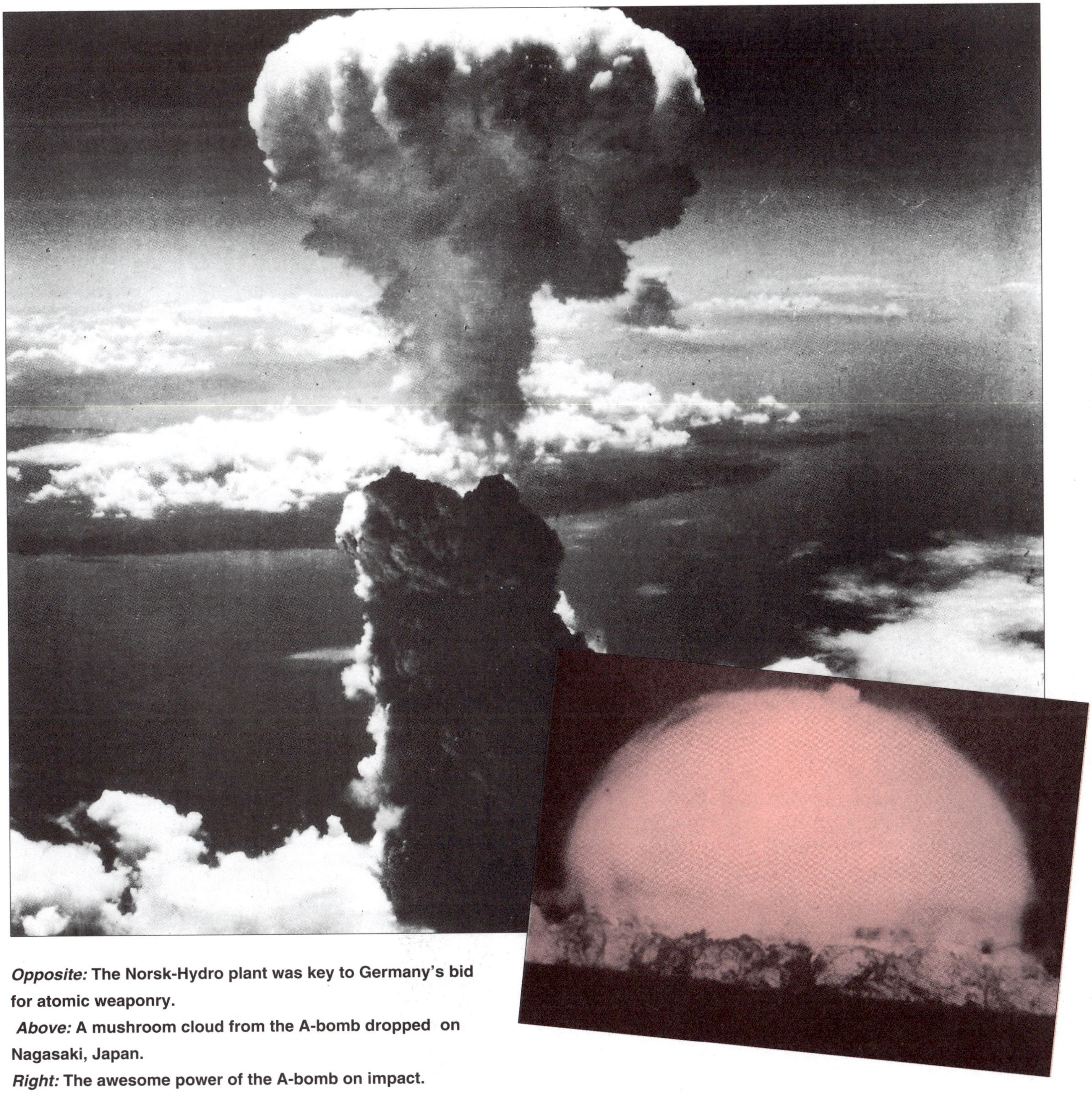

Opposite: The Norsk-Hydro plant was key to Germany's bid for atomic weaponry.

Above: A mushroom cloud from the A-bomb dropped on Nagasaki, Japan.

Right: The awesome power of the A-bomb on impact.

together with some of the surrounding territory,' the letter warned.

It was Einstein's theory of relativity published in 1905 that had enabled physicists to embark on the trail of the nuclear bomb.

ADVISORY BODY

After receiving the warning in August 1939, even before the outbreak of hostilities in Europe, Roosevelt decided to appoint an Advisory Committee on Uranium that year. Its report made worrying reading. A bomb of the nature and power predicted by Einstein was indeed a possibility and, in the wrong hands, it could bring unprecedented devastation to the world.

Albert Einstein's 1905 theory of relativity set physicists on the trail of the nuclear bomb

Even so, the Western nations were slow to make a concerted response to the issue. It wasn't until May 1941 that the US government set up an Office of Scientific Research and Development under the leadership of Dr Vannevar Bush. His brief was to channel all available resources into the field of nuclear research.

A report by Bush in March 1942 was sufficient to convince Roosevelt to launch a programme which would result in the construction of the first atomic bomb. It was called the

Below: The men of the University of Chicago research group gathered from all over the free world. These were the scientists who finally found the key to the nuclear age.

Manhattan Project and its very existence was kept as secret as any spy or security network.

At this stage, scientists knew little about the properties of uranium and its derivatives, the isotope U235 and plutonium. One of the biggest problems was finally solved by Italian professor Enrico Fermi in December 1942.

Fermi led a group of scientists who managed at last to control a nuclear chain reaction. They did it by using an atomic pile, another term for a nuclear reactor, built of layers of graphite and uranium on the football field of the University of Chicago.

A uranium nucleus was split when it was bombarded with a neutron. The resulting surge of nuclear energy was accompanied by free neutrons. These in turn split the nuclei and the process was repeated. It was the first man-made self-sustaining chain reaction of its kind in history.

The experiment was a triumph. Mindful of the secrecy surrounding the project, Nobel prize-winning physicist Arthur Compton sent the

> ***Many nuclear scientists had been forced to leave Germany because they were Jewish or anti-Nazi***

following cable to colleague James B. Conant: 'The Italian Navigator has just landed in the New World. The Natives are friendly.'

By now the Allies had decided to pool their scientific resources and all scientists of repute from the assembled countries were combining their brain power to produce the first atomic bomb.

Ironically, many were Germans who had been squeezed out of their homeland because they were Jewish or were suspected of having anti-Nazi sympathies.

Meanwhile in Germany scientists were still striving to gain the upper hand in the nuclear race. The invasion of Norway had provided them with the leg-up they needed.

HEAVY WATER

In France physicists working under Frederic Joliot-Curie had been experimenting with atomics using 'heavy water'. With the chemical name of D20, 'heavy water' is deuterium oxide, a form of water that has been infused with hydrogen with a boiling point of 101.42 degrees Centigrade. Nowadays it is used as a moderator and coolant in some nuclear reactors. Back then, it was produced only at the Rjukan dam in Norway.

As Germans closed in, Joiliot-Curie dispatched his close aide Hans von Halban to England with the French stocks of heavy water. A team of British and French scientists continued his work at Cambridge University until the centre of nuclear research moved to America.

With the heavy water plant, called Norsk-Hydro, in German hands, the British realised the threat. There was even more concern when the plant's production target for heavy water was raised from 3,000 pounds a year in 1942 to 10,000 pounds. It was a cue for action.

The plant nestled in the mountains of southern Norway amid dense forest. An initial plan to put it out of action with a team of commandos flown in by glider was thwarted when the light planes crashed.

As it was thought to be too difficult to bomb, six Norwegians were trained by Britain's Special Operations Executive to attack the dam.

The team, codenamed 'Gunnerside', was dropped into a remote region of Norway where they were greeted by a three-man advance party, 'Swallow'.

Clad in white camouflage suits, they skied cross-country to the dam to embark on their mission.

With great difficulty they scaled the plant, broke into the key installation and planted their explosives. They narrowly escaped before the

Above: **Physicist Dr Ernest Orlando Lawrence, of America, was one of the men who probed the workings of the atom in the development of the A-bomb.**

PATTON

US General George Patton won his reputation for revelling in warfare after making comments like: 'Compared to war, all other forms of human endeavour shrink to insignificance. God, how I love it.' He also wrote to his wife: 'Peace is going to be hell on me.'

Below: **Norsk-Hydro, the Norwegian centre of production for heavy water, was comprehensively bombed to put an end to its activities.**

blast which wrecked the tanks containing the precious heavy water. With the exception of two men left as a rearguard, the two teams fled to neutral Sweden.

On 16 November 1943 the dam came under attack from USAF B-17 Flying Fortresses

Despite this setback, the Germans were not finished yet. It took them months but they recovered and again stockpiled heavy water.

With a second sabotage operation deemed too dangerous, it was down to Allied bombers to wipe out the target. On 16 November 1943, the dam came under attack from a host of B-17 Flying Fortresses which showered it with heavy bombs.

BLOWN UP ON LAKE

While much of the site was wrecked, the last stocks of heavy water remained intact in specially built heavy duty concrete bunkers.

Scientists decided to move these remaining supplies to the comparative safety of Germany. The journey included a ferry crossing over one of Norway's deep lakes. The two men who had remained in Norway following the commando expedition earlier in the year were able to lead a team which put explosive charges in the bowels of the boat.

It was another flawless operation. As the ferry approached the deepest

point of the lake, the bombs went off and the ferry capsized. Although 26 passengers were killed, the Norwegian Resistance had nevertheless managed to end Hitler's foray into the field of nuclear weapons.

VON BRAUN

Frustrated by Allied action, Hitler lost interest in the nuclear race and concentrated all technical resources on his other secret weapons, the V-bombs. It left German scientists like Werner Heisenberg and Wernher von Braun tantalisingly close to cracking the nuclear code – but thankfully not quite close enough.

In America, unhindered by enemy operations and with considerably more cash at their disposal, Allied scientists were making great strides.

Even so, it wasn't until 16 July 1945 that the plutonium bomb 'Fat Man' was detonated at Los Alamos in New Mexico and the assembled scientists knew they were ready to enter the nuclear age. In charge of the project was Dr J. Robert Oppenheimer.

Above: **The Rjukan dam in southern Norway.**

Right: **The US plutonium bomb 'Fat Man' was tested here in the desert at Los Alamos, New Mexico.**

It was too late to have any effect in the war in Europe. That had ended in May 1945 shortly after the suicide of Hitler. But it was to have telling consequences on the conflict in the Pacific. Japan would not surrender, and the Allies feared a huge loss of life if the war dragged on for much longer while the Japanese mainland was liberated.

Tokyo finally agreed to a surrender with terms acceptable to the Allies after two atomic bombs had been dropped, one on Hiroshima and another on Nagasaki.

The secrets of the bomb were closely guarded to preserve world security. Yet although none of its nationals were working on the Manhattan Project, Russia was soon in possession of its ingredients and construction method.

No one gave the Russians more atomic secrets than German refugee Emil Klaus Julius Fuchs, a communist who had sought asylum in Britain when Hitler came to power in 1933. He gained a doctorate at Edinburgh University and afterwards worked in scientific research.

Like other German nationals in Britain when war broke out, Fuchs was interned as an 'alien' and shipped to Canada. On the way there his boat was torpedoed by a roaming U-boat and he was lucky to escape with his life.

Above: **After his release from a British jail, Fuchs flew to East Berlin where he was greeted by nephew Klaus Kittowski (*right*), and later reunited with his father Emil.**

By 1941 the British authorities were convinced he posed no threat and Fuchs returned to a job in the war effort. Poorly paid, it nevertheless required him to be vetted by security chiefs – this caused no difficulties.

On 7 August 1942 Fuchs became a British citizen. Yet he was already betraying the nation he swore allegiance to by passing information to the Russians.

He stepped up his efforts on behalf of Stalin when he was posted to the US to work on the nuclear devices.

LOS ALAMOS

Now his spymaster was the notorious Russian vice-consul Anatoli Yakovlev and his main regular contact a respected biochemist by the name of Harry Gold.

Fuchs was one of the privileged few to witness the Los Alamos test as he now worked alongside the man known as the father of the atom bomb, Dr Robert Oppenheimer.

Afterwards, Fuchs had a fat dossier of facts to hand over to his Soviet friends, including details of the new bomb's design and the components necessary for its construction.

At the end of World War II, Fuchs came home to work at Harwell on Britain's nuclear initiative. He even represented Britain at a 1947 conference in Washington, arguing that information about the nuclear industry given out to the Western public should be restricted.

In the same year he first accepted money from the Soviets for the nuggets he passed on. He was paid £100 for inside information on Windscale, Britain's new nuclear reactor plant in the north-west.

Little did he know his treachery had at last been detected. The clues left by Russian negotiators and in radio messages intercepted by America identified the traitor as someone who came from Britain and had witnessed the testing at Los Alamos. Fuchs was chief suspect but security investigators didn't have sufficient grounds to nail him.

FUCHS CONFESSES

In October 1949 Fuchs made an appointment with Harwell's security officer, Wing Commander Henry Arnold, with a 'personal problem'. Clearly troubled by his treachery, he said he was worried that he might became a target for Russian espionage attempts and was prepared to resign. It was the signal that the security chief had been waiting for.

An accomplished interrogator was dispatched to Harwell and, during the third interview, Fuchs admitted to his links with the Russians. His confession ultimately led him to the dock of the infamous No 1 Court at the Old Bailey where he admitted breaching the Official Secrets Act.

◆ EYE WITNESS ◆

Following the atomic bomb blasts Emperor Hirohito broadcast on the radio for the first time to his people.

"We, the Emperor, have ordered the Imperial Government to notify the four countries, the United States, Great Britain, China and the Soviet Union, that We accept their Joint Declaration. To ensure the tranquility of the subjects of the Empire and share with all the countries of the world the joys of co-prosperity, such is the rule that was left to Us by the Founder of the Empire of Our Illustrious Ancestors which We have endeavoured to follow. Today, however, the military situation can no longer take a favourable turn and the general tendencies of the world are not to our advantage either. What is worse, the enemy, who has recently made use of an inhuman bomb, is incessantly subjecting innocent people to grievous wounds and massacre. The devastation is taking on incalculable proportions. To continue the war under these conditions would not only lead to the annihiliation of Our Nation but the destruction of human civilisation as well."

Judge Lord Chief Justice Goddard had a tough rebuke for Fuchs:

'You took advantage of the privilege of asylum which has always been the boast of this country to people persecuted in their own country for their political opinions. You betrayed the hospitality and protection given to you by the greatest treachery.'

Fuchs was jailed for 14 years. On 12 February 1951 he was stripped of his British citizenship

Fuchs was jailed for 14 years. On 12 February 1951 he was stripped of his British citizenship. Eight years later when he was released from Wakefield jail, he chose to leave Britain for East Berlin. Ultimately, he became director of the East German Central Institute for Nuclear Physics at Rossendorf, near Dresden.

His seven-year betrayal of Britain and the USA undoubtedly did a great deal to advance Russia's knowledge of nuclear weaponry. Yet Fuchs was not the only scientist in the West who betrayed nuclear secrets to Stalin.

Soviet spy chief General Pavel Sudoplatov has alleged in his memoirs that Dr Oppenheimer himself, the man who led the Allied atomic bomb programme, was also guilty of spilling closely guarded secrets to the Russians.

Given the world order at the time, it is not altogether surprising that both Fuchs and Oppenheimer were prepared to assist Stalin.

PRO-COMMUNISTS

The pre-war prejudices against Communism had been cast aside in 1941 when Russia became one of the Allies and fought so bravely to repel the Nazis from its soil. And the Red Army played no small part in the downfall of Hitler, suffering millions of casualties in the process.

Those who harboured socialist sympathies were delighted to see communist Russia and capitalist America pulling together to achieve a common goal. This rose-tinted view was even shared by President Roosevelt who sincerely believed the end of the war would mark a new era of co-operation between the victors.

Right: **The A-bomb which was later to devastate Nagasaki, shown here in preparation on the island of Tinian the day before it was dispatched.**

EYE WITNESS

In the general election of 26 July 1945, Churchill was defeated in favour of Labour's Clement Attlee. Although wounded by the blow, Churchill spoke these words, alluding to the existence of the atomic bomb.

'The decision of the British people has been recorded in the votes counted today. I have therefore laid down the charge which was placed upon me in darker times. I regret that I have not been permitted to finish the work against Japan. For this, however, all plans and preparations have been made and the results may come much quicker than we have hitherto been entitled to expect. Immense responsibilities abroad and at home fall upon the new Government and we must all hope that they will be successful in bearing them.'

Sudoplatov, the man who organised Trotsky's murder, recalls how Oppenheimer condoned the exchange of information with Russian scientists before the end of the war. Following the war, Oppenheimer opposed the development of the hydrogen bomb. In 1954 he was branded a security risk by Senator Joseph McCarthy, the US politician who conducted a witch hunt against suspected left-wingers.

These were the days before the Iron Curtain when Stalin's empire-building was not entirely obvious. The men who handed over atomic secrets almost certainly never considered the gravity of their actions until the full extent of Stalin's brutal imperialism became clear.

AFTERMATH OF WAR

World War II had brought with it widespread death, starvation, homelessness, unmitigated misery and horror for millions. When peace broke out, none of that changed overnight.

For all the fighting nations, there was no time to lick their wounds. The immediate priority was to revive and reorganise in haste to lay the foundations for the future. It was to be a haphazard path to peace, however.

An estimated 50 million people had perished. Some countries suffered far more deaths than others. The Soviet Union was left mourning no fewer than 14 million people, only half of whom were fighting men – the other half were non-combatant civilians.

Poland had incurred grievous losses – approximately six million, around a fifth of her pre-war population. France lost half a million, Italy 330,000 and Holland was bereft of 200,000, most of whom were civilians killed in bombing raids or through deportation.

Britain lost 244,000 servicemen, and 60,000 civilians on the home front. America emerged unscathed on the home front but lost 292,000 servicemen overseas.

Britain lost 244,000 servicemen and an additional 60,000 people on the home front

Commonwealth countries had thousands of troops killed in action. Canada lost 37,000 men, India 24,000, Australia 23,000, New Zealand 10,000 and South Africa 6,000. Chinese losses were incalcuably high and continued as a civil war which had been raging before Japanese involvement in 1931 resumed.

Aggressors Germany and Japan had been severely battered. Four million German servicemen died for their Führer while 593,000 civilians were fatally wounded in Allied air attacks. Japanese casualties in the field alone amounted to 1.2 million. In addition, their countries were left with perhaps the worst battle scars and were now under occupation.

REFUGEES

In Europe the problem of homelessness was particularly acute. Air raids had accounted for many houses and flats, leaving the native populations in difficulty.

Also, there were refugees released from labour camps which had been set up throughout the Reich who now had no place to go. Many wished to avoid returning to the East for fear of coming into Stalin's clutches. The dispossessed were hungry and desperate people. There were many who were seeking personal revenge against the defeated Germans. They became a major security consideration for the occupying forces.

The situation was exacerbated in Germany by the flight of its population in the east when the Red Army approached. As many as a million died during the early months of 1945 when the flight from Stalin's vengeful troops began in earnest.

More Germans were expelled from eastern Europe and unceremoniously dumped in the British zone when peace broke out. The German population east of the Elbe was forcibly reduced from 17 million to 2,600,000. The number of displaced persons within the British zone of Germany was judged to top 2,460,000. That included 464,000 French people, 219,000 Belgians and 151,000 Dutch people all heading

Opposite: **Some children study the small print ahead of the signing of the United Nations Charter in San Francisco in 1945.** ***Below:*** **Less than five years after the end of World War II, trouble flared between the super powers in Korea.**

THE BATTLE OF BERLIN, APRIL 1945

In April 1945 Marshall Zhukov began preparations for the Red Army's final push on Berlin. Konev's 1st Ukrainian Front made for the Neisse River, Rokossovsky's 2nd Belorussian Front went to the northern bank of the River Oder, while Zhukov's own 1st Belorussians held the line along the Oder opposite Berlin. Together the three Soviet Fronts comprised no fewer than 2,500,000 men, 6,250 tanks, 7,500 aircraft and 41,600 artillery pieces. Berlin had already been bombed almost every night since 1 February, and then at dawn on 16 April the attack began in earnest. On 19 April the 1st Belorussian Front broke through the German defences and reached the outskirts of Berlin on the following day.

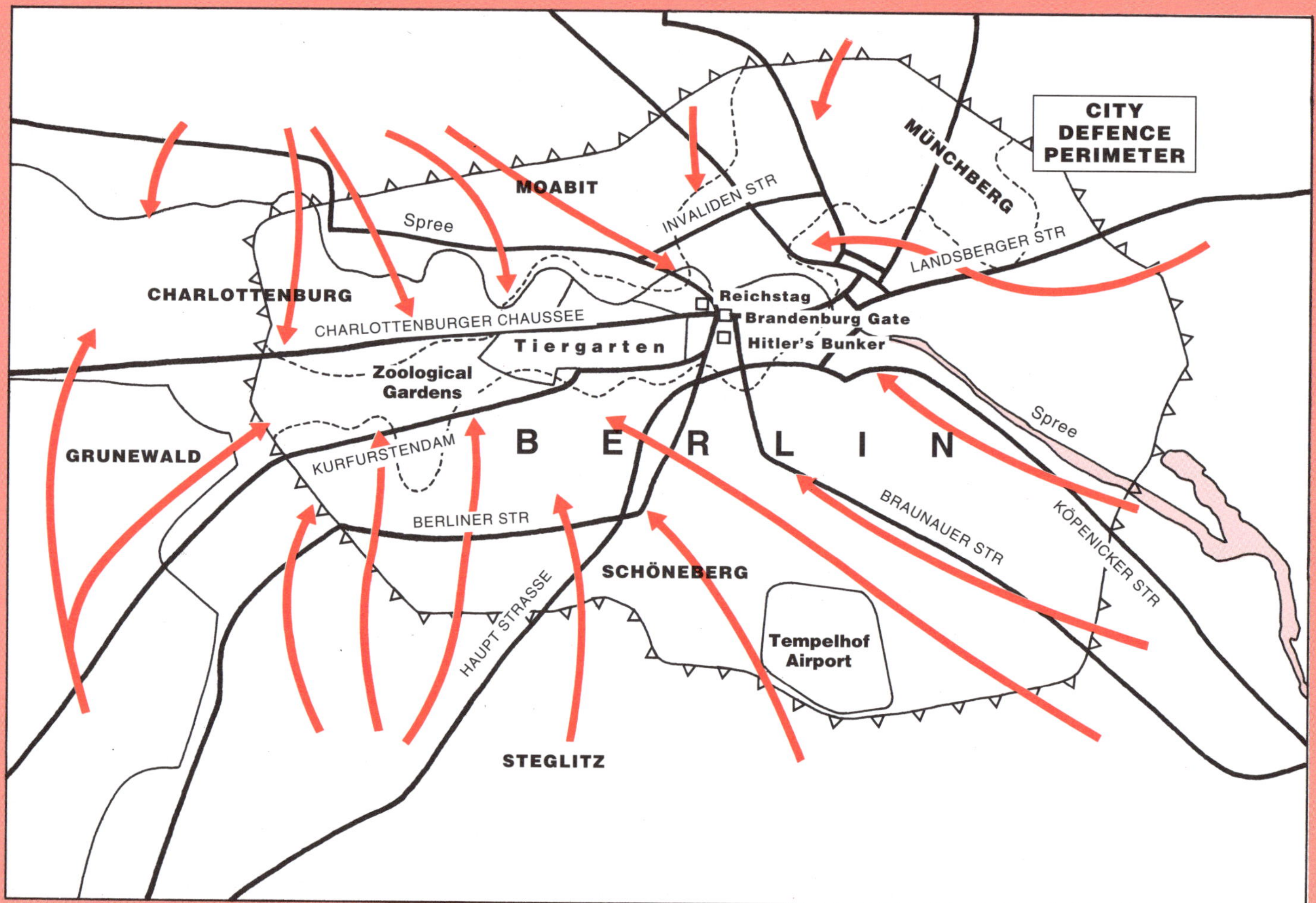

west and 580,000 Poles, 121,000 Russians and 422,000 Czechs destined to travel east.

UNITED NATIONS

Given the mighty bulge in population which had occurred in a country with a devastated economy, there was immense difficulty in feeding everyone. The aim was to give the Germans smaller rations so that those who had been starved for months and years at their hands could get better. Consequently, Germans were allowed about 12 ounces of bread a day, 10 ounces of potatoes but less than one ounce of meat and only one half ounce of fat and sugar. Also, the onus was put on the German people to supply the food needed for themselves and the displaced people inside their borders.

Fortunately the United Nations was already up and running although it wasn't formally launched until 24 October 1945. It had been started in 1944 after a series of conferences in Washington which resulted in a governing charter, and hoped to succeed where its predecessor, the League of Nations, had failed in preserving peace and fostering co-operation between nations. There were 51 founder member states.

From its Relief and Rehabilitation Administration came clothing, food and medical supplies which averted a crisis that could have enveloped Europe in its first few faltering months of peace.

As the victors prepared for peace, they looked towards the agreements drawn up at the Yalta conference held before the end of hostilities which had been duly ratified in Potsdam.

At Yalta were Churchill, Roosevelt and Stalin, the trio of leaders who had seen through the war

Even between the two conferences, held only months apart, the tensions between the Allies had perceptibly increased. At Yalta were Churchill, Roosevelt and Stalin, the trio of Allied leaders who had seen through the war.

POTSDAM

Before Potsdam, which was held in July 1945, Churchill had been replaced as British prime minister by Clement Attlee. Roosevelt had died, so President Truman represented America. The accord that existed between the original three seemed to have been diminished, not only because the new leaders were far less accommodating towards Stalin but also because of a growing intransigence in the Russian leader.

Stalin broadly mistrusted the intentions of Britain and France as the hostilities drew to a close. Throughout the conflict, he had felt that they were dragging their feet on military obligations in order to let Russia bear the main brunt of the German war machine.

Given the agonies inflicted by Germany on Russia, he was in no mood to compromise. He wanted enormous reparations levied against Germany of a type that would make it impossible for the country to be viable again for years. But President Truman wouldn't hear of this, because he was determined that the vanquished countries should have

NAZI WEALTH

Hitler's own attempts to dabble in the world of art were doomed to failure. He was twice turned down for Vienna's Academy of Fine Arts on account of the poor quality of his drawings. Yet his aspirations did not change. Now he decided, as Führer, to become a patron of the arts. Those fine pieces that he gathered around himself were looted from homes, galleries and museums all over the world.

His lieutenants also took their cue from Hitler. Through the ranks there was wholesale theft from the cities, towns and villages swallowed up by the Reich. When it became clear Germany was going to lose the war, much of the prized art was spirited out of the country to languish in the bank vaults of South America, Switzerland and the Arab countries. The proceeds from the plunder were used by ODESSA, the organisation which helped SS men evade justice and which still operates to this day.

Of course, many items have been recovered. In caches around Europe, the Allies discovered treasures worth millions of pounds. As recently as 1983 60 tonnes of gold taken from Rome Central Bank were discovered down the well of a monastery in northern Italy.

However, experts still believe there is some £50 billion worth of bullion and other valuables secreted away. The knowledge of much of its whereabouts died with those who were killed in the final months and weeks of the war. The rest continues to finance the existence of war criminals in hiding. Not a single German was charged after the hostilities. They got away with daylight robbery.

Right: **Churchill, Roosevelt and Stalin mapped out the defeat of Germany and Japan and much of the future of the world when they met at Yalta in February 1945.**

their part to play in the future of a safe and secure world.

Nevertheless, the spheres of influence for each of the victorious countries had been previously agreed and would be kept to.

The countries in the East were to fall under Russian domination, this being rubber stamped by the Allies

Under the Yalta treaty the countries in the East were to fall under Russian domination

even though it meant an ardently anti-Communist country like Poland being put into the hands of Stalin.

Germany was sectioned off into four, one piece each to America, Britain, France and Russia. A similar arrangement was made for the capital, Berlin. The Western nations decided Russia was behaving furtively and posed a threat to the rest of Europe. In 1946, Churchill spoke about the seriously deteriorating relations with Stalin on a visit to the US:

'Nobody knows what Soviet Russia and its Communist International organisation intends to do in the immediate future or what are the limits, if any, of their expansive and proselytizing tendencies. From Stettin on the Baltic to Trieste on the Adriatic, an iron curtain has descended across the continent.'

IRON CURTAIN

With the weight of Russia on one side, America determined to counter the balance to halt the suspected spread of communism. A civil war was raging in Greece between the Royalists, who had been receiving British aid, and the Communists. It caused appalling misery for civilians

◆ EYE WITNESS ◆

Edward Howe witnessed the liberation of a region of Yugoslavia where Tito's men had been fighting alongside the Red Army.

'Discipline among the Yugoslav Partisans had been strict and imposed with a rod of iron. Drunkeness, theft and promiscuousness with the opposite sex were all crimes punishable by death – in my experience there were no occasions that merited such drastic treatment. Pride in serving with the Partisans, the honour of the unit, and the fanatical zeal whipped up by military and political leaders alike had created a code that was self imposed and made individuals reject any form of indulgence. It was religious in its inspiration and fervour. Also, it was a code based on what they understood the Russians themselves to follow. They expected to find a spiritual affinity with the Russians.

Instead they found the Russians a swashbuckling, hard-living, hard-drinking, hard-swearing horde with no thoughts of politics and absolutely no understanding of Yugoslav struggles and achievements. To the majority of the Red Army men, Yugoslavia was just another stretch of country, indistinguishable from Rumania or Hungary, that separated them from wringing Hitler and every other German's neck.

There was a feeling of apprehension in the air about the future. People the world over are the same. After the war had rolled past, incurably optimistic, they expect life to revert back immediately to the golden days of peace just as though nothing had happened in between. Even more amazingly, they become hysterically put out when they find that the immediate post fighting period is worse, much worse, than the oppressed days of foreign occupation.'

Left: **After the defeat of Germany there were a few months in Berlin when the Allied leaders were all hailed as heroes. But acrimony between them soon set in.**

still reeling from the atrocities committed against the Jewish and partisan populations by the Germans. In 1947 when Britain could no longer afford to maintain a presence in Greece, America stepped in with troops and cash.

George Marshall believed only a strong Europe could resist the tide of communism

George Marshall, US Secretary of State, believed only a strong Europe could resist the tide of communism. Accordingly, he set in motion a plan to give food, fuel, raw materials and machinery to all European countries struggling to get on their feet once more. To distribute this aid the Organisation for European Economic Co-operation was formed in 1948. It comprised 16 member countries.

MARSHALL AID

The Marshall Aid plan was viewed by the Russians as empire building of the worst order by America and they in turn exerted pressure on countries in their own sphere of influence to turn down US offers of assistance. Only Yugoslavia defied Russian wishes and took advantage of the Marshall Plan, its leader Tito thus carving for himself an independence unknown in the Communist world.

Already it was clear that a vast gulf had opened up between the former allies. In March 1948 when the Western Allies decided to unite the divided zones of Germany, Russia reacted with menace. West Berlin, in the heart of East Germany, was suddenly isolated as Russia barricaded roads and railways into parts of the city under British, American and French control. Refusing to back down, the Western nations airlifted supplies to West Berlin daily for more than a year. It wasn't until secret negotiations in the spring of 1949

Below: **Allied planes flew in essential supplies to West Berlin for almost a year after the Soviet Union cut off land access routes to the western part of the city.**

ONE PENN

CADBURY means QUALITY

WEATHER Light, variable winds: fair; rather warm.

Daily Worker

No. 4336 FRIDAY, JULY 27, 1945

"Lettuce" use Sifta

THE PEOPLE SWEEP LABOUR TO POWER

Big Majority Over All Other Parties: Tories Are Routed

IN THE MOST SENSATIONAL ELECTION IN BRITAIN'S WHOLE HISTORY, THE PEOPLE HAVE SWEPT LABOUR TO GOVERNMENTAL POWER WITH A CLEAR MAJORITY OVER ALL OTHER PARTIES.

After more than five years of battle against Fascism in Europe, the British people have turned their attention to the Tories and routed them at the polls.

The state of parties at the end of yesterday's declarations—with 13 results to be announced later—was this :—

Labour	377	Communist	2
Tory, Lib. Nat. & Nat.	204	Common Wealth and I.L.P.	4
Liberal	10	Independent	10

AFTER THE PEOPLE'S VICTORY

Victory in Figures

Gains and losses at time of going to press were :—

Conservative gains 7, losses 178; National, nil, 2; Liberal-National, 1, 16; total for Government, losses, 196.

Labour, 207, 4; Liberal, 3, 10; Communist, 1, nil; Independent, 2, 10; total Opposition, gains, 213.

The aggregate votes cast in the constituencies where returns had been made were as follows :—

Conservative, 8,004,615; Liberal National, 140,221; National, 702,069. Total for the Government,

8,846,905.

Labour, 10,843,228; Liberal, 2,060,387; Communist, 74,540; Independent, 389,450. Total for Opposition,

13,530,828.

Two Communists In the New House

Daily Worker Reporter

Above: **British politics changed when Churchill was ousted and the Labour Party won the July 1945 general election.**

that the stalemate was broken though Germany remained in two parts with a Western enclave in Berlin in the middle of the communist East.

Out of this crisis grew the North Atlantic Treaty Organisation, a defensive grouping including America, Britain, France, Canada and other European and Scandinavian countries. Other countries sought membership during its history and agreed to abide by its main rule, that they would come to the aid of any member state which was attacked. Russia saw this as a direct threat and set up its own military agreement with other communist countries, called the Warsaw Pact.

The Cold War began after the Berlin Airlift in 1948 and continued right up until 1990

This crisis, coupled with an arms build-up during which each side stockpiled deterrent weapons, led to the Cold War between Russia and the East and America and the West being frozen into place. This stand-off between the superpowers lasted until Mikhail Gorbachev came to power in Russia in 1985, after which he actively supported the Strategic Arms Limitation Talks (SALT) which were already in progress and instituted further measures of his own to scale down hostilities.

The Cold War finally came to a close in 1990 following the momentous political changes made in the Eastern bloc.

Despite the depths to which Germany had plummeted in those dark days straight after the armistice, it wasn't long before at least part of the defeated nation was back on its feet. Thanks to the American aid package, which had been lent in no small part to make West Germany a strong buffer between communist Eastern Europe and the free West, production levels by 1950 matched those of 1938. From that point, West Germany built a strong economy and developed an enviable track record for its industry.

◆ EYE WITNESS ◆

Swedish-born Nels Olson, 72, from Chicago, USA, was a gunner in the US Navy Armed Guard, who later served in the Pacific at the time of the Japanese surrender.

"My war ended in the Pacific. I arrived on the island of Okinawa two or three weeks after the Japanese surrender. All the guys wore guns when they went ashore but there were no problems. The Japanese bowed to us whenever they saw us. It was like they went out of their way to show they did not want to fight.

For a country that caused us such problems I was amazed at how primitive some of the people were. I once had to supervise the unloading of coal from a cargo ship. They did it by sending men on board with two buckets strapped to their shoulders. It was amazing to watch."

As if to emphasise the division, in 1961 the communist leaders built a wall between East and West Berlin to cage its people in. In the years that followed, many East Berliners perished attempting to cross to the free West. It stood as a sorry tribute to the grimy side of communism for nearly 30 years until Germany reunited in 1990 and the wall was torn down.

POSTWAR EUROPE

Postwar Italy struggled to keep an even keel. King Umberto II was ousted by referendum in 1946. Yet successive republican Italian governments have been unable to find a reliable formula for stability. Amid unending allegations of corruption, Italy's economy has remained unstable while socially the country has suffered from bombs, kidnapping and other forms of terrorism.

France, meanwhile, had its own problems. Torn by a wartime record of honour and shame in almost equal measures, there was clearly going to be difficulty in restoring national pride.

Leader of the Free French, General Charles de Gaulle was determined to instil that sense of greatness back into France. However, he left power in 1946 and didn't return until 1958 when he set himself on a collision course with Britain and America, the two powers which had treated him with great caution and suspicion during war time.

Now under a Labour government, Britain nationalised industry and launched a welfare state

Yet despite de Gaulle's hostility to the USA, it was American help which enabled France to become a modern and viable state by the mid-1950s.

Now under a Labour government, Britain set about nationalising many of its services and industries and launched a welfare state. Still, it did not enjoy the same speedy rate of recovery as its fellow European nations. Food rationing remained in place for some years and there was a shortage of quality housing. Most people found their existences dreary.

SUEZ CRISIS

Winston Churchill was at the helm again following the 1951 election and remained in charge until 1954 when Anthony Eden took over. Eden was compelled to resign after sending the British army into Suez when the canal was nationalised by Egyptian leader Nasser in 1956. The move, made in tandem with the French, earned international rebuke.

Like France, Britain gave independence to many of its colonies, primarily India which won its status in 1947 after a protracted campaign. This was perhaps the more successful side to post-war foreign policy.

Britain had supported the Jewish demand for a home nation in Palestine. Yet, as administrator of Palestine, it had sympathy with the anxious Arab population too. Consequently, Britain refused to raise the limit set on Jewish immigration into the area following the war for fear of sparking an Arab uprising.

Instead, it was the Jews who rebelled with a terrorist campaign which began in October 1945. By the following year some 80,000 British troops were tied down in Palestine attempting to keep the peace.

In 1947 the UN proposed to run the area as two separate states, one Jewish, the other Arab. Consequently, the state of Israel was created in 1948 with the rest of Palestine being divided between Jordan and Eygpt. The disaffection thereby created among Palestinian Arabs festered until it finally erupted into violence which manifested itself throughout the following decades. Only at the start of the 1990s did the problem appear to have a resolution.

Troops were also sent into action in Malaya, Indo-China and Indonesia as Britain policed trouble spots which flared around the world.

In 1973 Britain at last signed its name to the European Economic Community which was created in 1957 following the Treaty of Rome. At the start the Community involved the Benelux countries, France, Italy and West Germany who, under the umbrella of the EEC or Common Market, aspired to closer co-operation and increased economic activity. By the time Britain joined, it was called the European Community. Since then several more countries in the region have joined the EC.

POSTWAR USSR

The Union of Soviet Socialist Republics remained under Stalin's control until his death in 1953. His ambition to extinguish Germany was thwarted and he was forced to

Below: **Trouble between Israelis and Arabs occurred for years after the creation of the Jewish state in 1948. In 1973 came the Yom Kippur War.**

content himself with looting industrial machinery from the regions his armies overran.

The dictator fostered imperialist aims and exerted an iron grip on the countries under the communist umbrella. Although many of his harsh internal measures were condemned by later Soviet regimes, at the time no one dared raise a voice of criticism.

GLASNOST

The Soviet government used its military might to crush the Hungarian Revolution of 1956 and the Czechoslovak steps towards liberation in 1968 went the same way. Following the policy of 'Glasnost' or 'openness' installed by Mikhail Gorbachev, the communist systems in the USSR and surrounding countries collapsed and were replaced by democracies. The USSR itself ceased to exist in December 1991. Most of the former Soviet republics became known as the Commonwealth of Independent States – the exceptions were Georgia and the three Baltic states.

Seeds were sown in World War II which were to have tragic consequences some 45 years later. When the Germans marched into Yugoslavia, they granted rule to the nationalistic Croatians called Ustashi. After themselves feeling marginalised since Yugoslavia was created at the end of World War I, they now chose to seek vengeance. Atrocities were committed by the Ustashi against Serbs, Jews and other races that made up the state.

Opposing the Germans and Ustashi were the Serbian Chetniks and communists led by Tito. Following the war, Tito seized control and operated a less restrictive version of communism in a united Yugoslavia, maintaining its position as a non-aligned country.

On Tito's death in 1980, the threads that held the country together began to unravel with individual groups setting up their own power bases. A decade after the death of the dictator, Yugoslavia split up into five republics. However, memories of wartime injustices emerged and, coupled with dissatisfaction about new frontiers, these bubbled up into civil war. There followed one of the bloodiest and most vicious civil conflicts of modern times with reprisal following hot on the heels of attack, involving Serbians, Croats and the minority Muslim population. All attempts by the international community to make peace seemed doomed to failure.

America emerged from World War II as the wealthiest of the participating nations and was thus able to lend assistance to many others. During the Cold War years, its policies were mostly marked by a strident opposition to communism, encapsulated in Joe McCarthy's Un-American Activities Committee which harassed suspected left-wingers from all parts of American society. This American abhorrence of communism led them to intervene in Korea in 1950, in Cuba in 1961 and most protractedly and disastrously in Vietnam in 1961.

Left: **Mao Tse-Tung won the civil war in 1949 and isolated China from the world.**

> ***Japan has emerged as one of the most successful postwar industrial nations***

Japan remained under US occupation until 1951 when the Emperor renounced his claims of divinity. Welcomed back into the international fold when it joined the UN in 1956, Japan has emerged as one of the most successful postwar industrial nations.

Fighting continued in China where a civil war – suspended following the Japanese invasion – began once more. Chiang Kai-Shek, the Chinese nationalist, was pitted against communist Mao Tse-Tung. Mao triumphed in 1949 and then ruled until his death in 1976. Afterwards there were alternate periods of liberalisation and repression, the most noted example of the latter being the massacre of thousands of students in Tiananmen Square in Beijing in 1989.

So World War II was not a war to end all wars. But while the world has been peppered with conflicts since 1945, it is a tribute to all those who died between 1939 and 1945 that no all-consuming conflict has since engulfed the globe.